GUNS&AMMO
MAGAZINE

The Shooter's Guide to

Classic Firearms

Stoeger Publishing Company — *Accokeek, Maryland*

StoegerBooks
Great Outdoor Books Since 1924

STOEGER PUBLISHING COMPANY
is a division of Benelli U.S.A.

Benelli U.S.A.
Vice President & General Manager:
   Stephen Otway
Vice President of Marketing & Communications:
   Stephen McKelvain

Stoeger Publishing Company
President: Jeffrey Reh
Managing Editor: Harris J. Andrews
Creative Director: Cynthia T. Richardson
Marketing & Communications Manager:
   Alex Bowers
Imaging & Pre-Press Manager: William Graves
National Sales Manager: Jennifer Thomas
Special Accounts Manager: Julie Brownlee
Publishing Assistants: Amy Jones, Amy Sargent
Copy Editor: Amy Jones
Proofreader: Amy Jones

Published by Stoeger Publishing Company
17603 Indian Head Highway, Suite 200
Accokeek, Maryland 20607

BK0606
ISBN-10: 0-88317-327-1
ISBN-13: 978-0-88317-327-5
Library of Congress Control Number: 2006923638

Manufactured in China.

Distributed to the book trade and
to the sporting goods trade by:
Stoeger Industries
17603 Indian Head Highway, Suite 200
Accokeek, Maryland 20607
301-283-6300   Fax: 301-283-6986
www.stoegerpublishing.com

OTHER PUBLICATIONS:

Shooter's Bible
   The World's Standard
   Firearms Reference Book
Gun Trader's Guide
   Complete Fully Illustrated
   Guide to Modern Firearms
   with Current Market Values

Hunting & Shooting:
The Bowhunter's Guide
Elk Hunter's Bible
High Performance
   Muzzleloading
   Big Game Rifles
High Power Rifle Accuracy:
   Before You Shoot
Hunt Club
   Management Guide
Hunting Whitetails
   East & West
Hunting the Whitetail Rut
Shotgunning for Deer
Taxidermy Guide
Tennessee Whitetails
Trailing the Hunter's Moon
The Turkey Hunter's
   Tool Kit: Shooting Savvy
The Ultimate in Rifle Accuracy
Whitetail Strategies

Firearms:
Antique Guns:
   A Collector's Guide
How to Buy & Sell Used Guns
Gunsmithing Made Easy
Model 1911: Automatic Pistol
Modern Beretta Firearms

Reloading:
The Handloader's Manual of
   Cartridge Conversions 3rd Ed.

Fishing:
Big Bass Zone
Catfishing:
   Beyond the Basics
Fishing Made Easy
Fishing Online:
   1,000 Best Web Sites
Flyfishing for Trout A-Z
Practical Bowfishing

Cooking Game:
The Complete Book of
   Dutch Oven Cooking
Healthy Game & Fish Meals
Wild About Freshwater Fish
Wild About Game Birds
Wild About Seafood
Wild About Venison
Wild About Waterfowl
World's Best Catfish Cookbook

Nature:
The Pocket Disaster
   Survival Guide
The Pocket Survival Guide
U.S. Guide to Venomous
   Snakes and Their Mimics

Fiction:
The Hunt
Wounded Moon

Nonfiction:
Escape In Iraq:
   The Thomas Hamill Story

GUNS&AMMO
MAGAZINE

Front cover:
The 9mm Browning Hi-Power automatic pistol, such as this
example manufactured by the John Inglis Company of Canada,
was carried by both Allied and Axis armed forces during World
War II. The rugged Hi-Power is still in service with military
and police forces worldwide.

Introduction

What constitutes a classic firearm? There are probably more opinions on that particular subject than one can possibly imagine. Assemble any group of firearms enthusiasts—collectors, hunters, target shooters, and a host of others—and there will probably be as many opinions as to what constitutes a "classic" as there are individuals.

There seem to be several significant definitions, however. A classic can be a weapon that represents a benchmark in firearms technology and development—a particular action, ignition system, style of rifling, or some other innovative design. These might include Winchester's landmark lever actions or the U.S. Army's M-1 Garand with its ingenious rotating bolt and semi-auto firing system. Other "classics" can include long arms or handguns that are treasured for their style, balance, dependability and all-around effectiveness—their utility and popularity so to speak. In this class the U.S. 1903 Springfield service rifle, the Sharps buffalo rifle, or the 1873 Colt Single-Action Army revolver come to mind. While yet other examples might be considered classics because of their association with great events—the Japanese Type 99 Arisaka rifle carried by seemingly invincible Japanese forces on their march of conquest across East Asia and the South Pacific, or

the legendary C.96 Mauser "Broomhandle," favored by Russian Bolsheviks and Chinese warlords alike.

Beginning in 1999, several of the technical editors at *Guns & Ammo* magazine created the "Classic Test" column, a regular feature that examined many of the world's "great" firearms that have come to be treasured by collectors, hunters, historians and gun enthusiasts. Authors Garry James, Jeff John, Phil Schreier, Payton Miller, Rick Hacker, Steve Comus, Phil Spangenberger, Wiley Capp, Dennis Adler, and J. Scott Rupp, bought, borrowed or drew on their own collections to put "shootable" examples of classic military and civilian firearms through their paces. Ammunition, sometimes rare and difficult to obtain, was collected and evaluated. The pieces were then tested for function, reliability, ease of use and accuracy, among other things, and the resulting articles provide the reader not only with technical evaluations, but with histories of the development and use of some of the world's most popular collectable and useful vintage firearms.

Collected in book form for the first time from the pages of *Guns & Ammo*, these "classic tests" will provide welcome information garnered by experts who actually took these classics to the firing line.

Contents

Classic Rifles 6

Classic Military Rifles

BRITISH MARTINI-HENRY — GARRY JAMES 8
U.S. SPRINGFIELD .45-70 TRAPDOOR — GARRY JAMES 12
GERMAN MODEL 71/84 MAUSER — GARRY JAMES 16
FRENCH MODEL 1886 LEBEL RIFLE — GARRY JAMES 20
BRITISH LONG LEE-ENFIELD — GARRY JAMES 24
MODEL 1909 ARGENTINE MAUSER — STEVE COMUS 28
MK III SHORT MAGAZINE LEE-ENFIELD — GARRY JAMES 32
WINCHESTER RUSSIAN MODEL 1895 — GARRY JAMES AND PHILIP SCHREIER 36
U.S. MODEL 1896 KRAG-JORGENSEN CARBINE — GARRY JAMES 40
JAPANESE TYPE 99 ARISAKA — STEVE COMUS 44
U.S. M 1 GARAND — GARRY JAMES 48
U.S. JOHNSON M 1941 — PAYTON MILLER 52

Classic Sporting Rifles

1878 SHARPS BORCHARDT — JEFF JOHN 56
WINCHESTER MODEL 1890 .22 WRF — JEFF JOHN 60
1903 SPRINGFIELD NRA SPORTER — GARRY JAMES 64
WINCHESTER MODEL 88 — STEVE COMUS 68
WINCHESTER MODEL 71 — RICK HACKER 72

Classic Pistols 76

Classic Shotguns 138

Index 160

Classic Rifles

Classic Military Rifles
British Martini-Henry

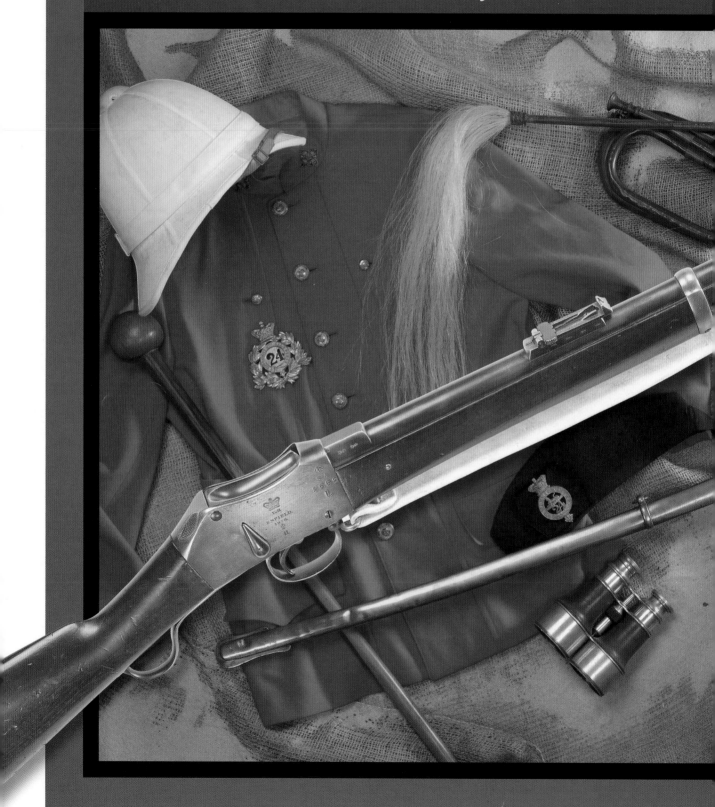

This rugged, reliable British single-shot rifle was used by regular and colonial forces worldwide.

It's interesting how motion pictures can affect the firearms market. There is no better case in point than the Martini-Henry/*Zulu* phenomenon. In 1964 Cy Endfield brought out a film extolling the exploits of a small contingent of British and Colonial troops at a mission station in South Africa who made a heroic stand against thousands of disciplined Zulu warriors.

This 1879 engagement, the Battle of Rorke's Drift, garnered more Victoria Crosses for its participants, per capita, than any other single engagement in British history. The film, *Zulu*, featured actors Stanley Baker, Michael Caine and Jack Hawkins, among others, though it could be said that the real star of the picture was the .577-.450 Martini-Henry rifle. It was showcased prominently and was given much credit for winning the day.

Almost as soon as the film appeared, interest in this heretofore obscure British military single-shot rifle began to increase—to the point where

THE MARTINI-HENRY RIFLE SAW SERVICE IN SUCH DISPARATE LOCALES AS CANADA, AFRICA, CHINA AND AUSTRALIA.

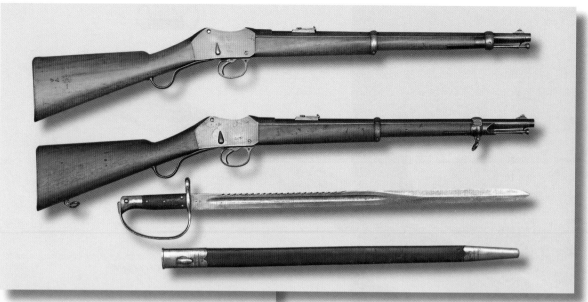

AS WELL AS AN INFANTRY VERSION, THE MARTINI-HENRY WAS MADE IN CAVALRY (TOP) AND ARTILLERY CARBINE VERSIONS (BELOW). THE LATTER IS PROBABLY THE SCARCEST OF THE THREE. THIS EXAMPLE WAS MADE BY W.J. JEFFERY & CO. FOR BRITISH VOLUNTEERS. ITS SWORD BAYONET HAS A SAWTOOTH EDGE FOR USE BY PIONEERS.

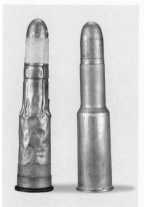

THE M-H CHAMBERED A POWERFUL .577-.450 BLACK POWDER ROUND. EARLY CARTRIDGES (LEFT) WERE MADE OF COILED BRASS FOIL WITH SEPARATE IRON BASES. AMMO USED FOR OUR EVALUATION (RIGHT) USED MODERN DRAWN BRASS CASES.

AMMUNITION FOR THE MARTINI-HENRY COULD BE LOADED AND EJECTED RAPIDLY. THE LOADING LEVER PROVIDED EXCELLENT LEVERAGE AND CASES WERE THROWN CLEAR OF THE RECEIVER.

today it is difficult to find a good Mark I or Mark II M-H in any kind of condition for anything approaching a realistic price. I was fortunate enough to buy a Mark II along with a Mark I Martini-Henry Cavalry Carbine and Artillery Carbine, and have probably turned down more offers for them than any other guns in my collection.

To be fair, the Martini-Henry has much more virtue than being just a pretty face on the screen. It was a robust, reliable, hard-hitting rifle that served British and Colonial troops around the world for several decades.

Its history actually began in America in the late 1860s where a falling-block, exposed hammer breechloader was contrived by gunmaker Henry O. Peabody. The "Peabody" was evaluated briefly by the U.S. Army and was actually issued by the State of Massachusetts.

Naturally Peabody was interested in overseas contracts and his system was widely exposed in Europe, where the Romanians and Turks thought highly enough of it to adopt it in 1868 and 1877, respectively. The Swiss were also quite taken with the gun, and they reworked it to a considerable degree, substituting an internal hammer and heavily reworking other parts of the mechanism. This "Martini" (named for the designer, Fredrich von Martini) eventually made its way to the British rifle trials where, after considerable testing, it was mated to a barrel with rifling devised by Alexander Henry.

The "Martini-Henry," as the rifle was now called, was chambered for a powerful .577-.450 round which employed a lengthened .577 Snider (the previous British service round) case, necked down to .45 caliber. These early Boxer rounds were of coiled brass foil, with separate black-painted iron bases. The 480-grain, paper-patched lead bullet was backed with 85 grains of black powder, which pushed it along at some 1,350 feet per second. A lighter carbine load was issued with a 405-grain bullet. The Boxer cartriges were fragile and the base could be ripped off by the extractor in an overheated rifle, so drawn brass cartridges were devised.

The Martini-Henry was strong and simple to operate. To work the action, one simply lowered a lever located beneath the wrist of the stock to drop the breechblock and expose the chamber. A round was manually inserted and the action closed. Opening the action again vigorously expelled the spent case and readied the piece for another round. Though the Martini-Henry did not have a safety, authorities added a tear-shaped cocking indicator on the side of the action.

In early tests it was found that if the shooter gripped the rifle in the usual manner with the thumb over the wrist of the stock, the gun's substantial recoil could cause the shooter's knuckle to be slammed into his nose. To alle-viate this problem, a knurled thumb rest was milled out of the top of the receiver.

The Martini-Henry infantry rifle was 54 inches long with a barrel of 32 inches. It weighed a well-balanced 9 pounds. Although authorities were disappointed with long-range accuracy, the rear ladder sight was graduated to an optimistic 1,450 yards. The front barley-corn sight also served as a bayonet stud for the "other ranks'" (enlisted men's) 21½-inch-long triangular bayonet. Sergeants were issued a 22½-inch yataghan-style sword bayonet, which snapped onto a stud on the right side of the front barrel band.

My own Martini, which we opted to use for our test piece, is a Mark II made in 1878. Original ammo is generally unshootable, though you can reload for the piece. Dave Cumberland of The Old Western Scrounger came to the rescue with some lovely new drawn-brass, Berdan-primed black powder loads featuring issue-style 480-grain lead bullets.

We took our Mark II to the range for a going over. Despite the gun's substantial heft, recoil was a tad on the stout side, though certainly not prohibitive. The trigger pull came in at a very crisp 9 pounds and the gun operated flawlessly, effectively ejecting the spent cases.

Accuracy was pretty ho-hum, with 100-yard groups coming in at between 6 and 8 inches. This is no fault of the ammo, as I have had simi-lar results with my handloads and some Kynoch smokeless loads in the past. One can't blame the rifling, either, as the bore was close to pristine. I guess this is just about all one can expect out of the old war-horse using military-style rounds.

THE STANDARD MARTINI-HENRY INFANTRY RIFLE HAD A 32-INCH BARREL, MEASURED 54 INCHES OVERALL AND WEIGHED SOME 9 POUNDS. BAYONETS INCLUDED A TRIANGU-LAR-MODEL FOR "OTHER RANKS" AND A WAVY-BLADED YATAGHAN-STYLE FOR SERGEANTS.

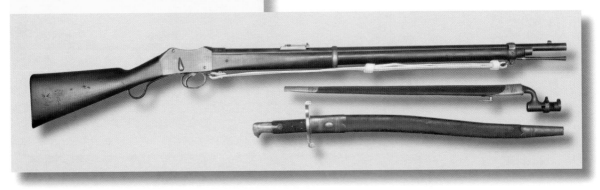

Classic Military Rifles
U.S. Springfield .45-70 Trapdoor

This classic breechloader remained in service for almost a half-century.

While the majority of battlefield casualties during the American Civil War were inflicted by muzzle-loading rifled muskets, scads of different types of breech-loading longarms, and a couple of repeaters, were also tested during the conflict—and were generally found to be superior to the older muzzle-loaders. In fact, breechloaders had been adopted as primary issue arms in some of the German states a decade or so prior to the War Between the States, and other countries, such as Britain and France, were making great strides in this area as well.

By 1864 it was recognized that breechloaders employing self-contained cartridges were the wave of the future, and the War Department set about investigating the situation. Ever economy-minded, authorities were really looking for a system in which the thousands of rifled muskets then in service could be readily converted to cartridge arms. As might be expected in the land of "Yankee ingenuity" scores of designs were submitted for testing. Of course, Americans were not the only ones concerned with saving money, and the British, for example, ended up adopting a conversion system for their Enfields devised by Jacob Snider of New York in 1866. Many inventors put forth their devices, but the Army threw in something of a ringer when it directed Erskin S. Allin, master armorer at Springfield Armory, to come up with plan of his own.

Many ideas were offered and rejected. When the smoke cleared, those of Henry O. Peabody and Christopher Spencer were decided to be superior to all others, despite the fact neither was suitable for altering the older muskets. Officialdom more or less shelved the findings and continued to look for the ideal conversion. The Allin system was the one finally chosen.

Originally it involved cutting away the top of the rifled musket barrel at the breech and affixing a "trap-door," which was hinged at the front and secured at the rear by a thumb-operated latch. This was found to be too delicate and the extractor less than efficient in pulling expended cases from the chamber. What finally emerged was an entirely satisfactory setup involving an entire breech mechanism screwed on the rear of the barrel. It contained the trapdoor, extractor and thumb catch. The rear hinge was beefed up and the extractor improved.

THE U.S. .45-70 TRAPDOOR RIFLE WAS HANDSOME, WELL-MADE AND SERVED IN VARIOUS CAPACITIES FOR OVER HALF A CENTURY. THIS MODEL 1889 RIFLE IS SHOWN WITH NEW YORK VOLUNTEER UNIFORM AND EQUIPMENT FROM THE SPANISH-AMERICAN WAR.

To load a Springfield Trapdoor, (1) put the gun on half-cock (2) lift up on the thumb latch (3) swing the breechblock open (4) insert a cartridge (5) close the block.

In 1865, "Allin's Alteration" was officially adopted. As it had a long firing pin traversing at an angle from the front of the block to the rear, where it could be struck by a modified musket hammer, the rifle was nicknamed the "Needle Gun"—not to be confused with the German Dreyse *Zundnadelgewehr* (needle gun) that preceded it by a couple of decades.

Caliber was initially .58, but a year later this was reduced to .50 by reaming out and sleeving the older muzzle-loading barrels. This Model 1866 rifle also had an improved breechblock, better extractor and a guard on the rear of the block that kept the hammer from striking the firing pin if the breech was not entirely closed. The centerfire cartridge chosen for the arm employed a 450-grain .50-caliber lead bullet backed by 70 grains of powder—the .50-70 Government.

Various models of .50-70 Allins were issued as rifles and carbines through 1873, but testing continued and, despite favorable reports garnered by Peabody, Sharps and Remington, it was felt the trapdoor system was efficient and reliable enough to undergo further revamping.

Following the lead of the military arms of other countries, the caliber was reduced from .50 to .45. The weapons were now manufactured from scratch. Instead of being finished in bright metal, the barrels and metal furniture were blued and the blocks case-hardened. Bullet weight for the rifle was 500 grains and for the lighter carbine, 405 grains. Cases were of copper composition and primed by the Benet internal system.

The guns were found to be accurate and reliable, though it was noted that sometimes the sharp blade of the extractor could cut through the soft copper case rim, lodging the shell in the chamber; it would have to be removed with a knife or similar implement. The .45-70 Trapdoor would go through a number of models and variations, generally involving breechblock and sight alterations.

The Model 1884 represented the high-water mark in the Trapdoor, and it was fitted with an extremely sophisticated Buffington rear sight that was easily adjusted for windage and elevation. While early model rifles were equipped with separate ramrods and triangular bayonets, the Model 1889 Springfield had a curious combination cleaning rod and bayonet, which could be pulled out from beneath the barrel. The gun could also take a standard socket bayonet if needed.

A TRAP IN THE 1889'S BUTTPLATE PROVIDES SPACE FOR A TAKEDOWN TOOL AND BROKEN SHELL EXTRACTOR.

Despite the fact that the U.S. Army went over to the Krag-Jorgensen bolt-action repeater in 1892, many Trapdoors were used in Cuba by volunteer units during the Spanish-American War. While they acquitted themselves reasonably well, they were certainly no match for the Spanish Mausers. Too, they were still using black-powder cartridges and the smoke both gave away position and obscured the enemy. When coming up against modern smokeless arms this put the volunteers at a disadvantage.

Still, the old .45-70s continued into service well into World War I, where they were used for drill purposes and as "fencing muskets" for bayonet practice. Finally, thousands were sold as surplus for very reasonable prices and provided many a poor civilian with a fairly reasonable hunting arm. The .45-70 itself is no slouch and is pretty much able to dispatch most North American game, within reasonable limitations.

Following World War II, it was not uncommon to see bins full of Trapdoor rifles and carbines at gunshops and surplus stores, selling for less than $5. I still remember some clever entrepreneurs who took Trapdoors and made lamps out of them, which sold (depending on whether you bought a single or triple-gun arrangement) for $29.95 to $59.95.

My evaluation Trapdoor was a Model 1889 rifle in extremely good condition. The bore was perfect and most of the finish remained, including the usually fragile case-hardening. The stock was deeply stamped with inspector's initials and the date "1891."

Chosen ammunition was Remington smokeless 405-grain SPs and 500-grain BP lead loads put together by my associate Jeff John. It should be noted: Never fire a Trapdoor with anything other than ammunition loaded to original or lighter specs! The action, while efficient, is not all that strong and beefed-up rounds are an invitation to disaster.

The rear sight was excellent, and I chose to shoot groups with the provided peep. Adjustments for range were easily effected.

Loading the gun is simple: Put the gun on half-cock, lift up the latch and swing the block forward. A case may be loaded into the breech. Close the block, cock the hammer, aim and fire. Ejection is accomplished by simply cocking and opening the block. The spring-loaded ejector finger tosses the case well clear of the action. This can all be accomplished in a few seconds, and the gun can be loaded and fired with great rapidity—as was discovered by the Sioux who faced early Allins at the Wagon Box fight near Bozeman, Montana, in 1867. The gun is very reliable and one can load and shuck shells with great ease.

Its old, curved steel buttplate, a throwback to Civil War-era rifled muskets, did little to ease recoil. Despite the gun's 8¼-pound heft, recoil with both smokeless and black powder loads was a bit stiff. Accuracy, especially with the proper 500-grain black powder loads, was excellent. I was able to achieve consistent 100-yard 2⅜-inch rested groups, though the gun had a tendency to shoot a tad high.

The fact that the Trapdoor system lasted in service for a half-century is a pretty good testimonial to an arm that was once considered to be something of a "stopgap" system.

This 11mm bolt-action repeater was one of Peter Paul Mauser's earliest and most successful designs.

Despite the fact that they thoroughly trounced Napoleon III's troops in the Franco-Prussian War, the Germans were not content to sit back and rest on their laurels. The Dreyse needle gun with which their troops were armed was, by the latter part of the 1860s, a delicate and creaky relic of times past. Immediately, German Chancellor Otto von Bismarck and his crew set about replacing their paper cartridge-eating dinosaur with a modern centerfire bolt gun designed by no less a person than Peter Paul Mauser.

The solid, well-built Model 1871 Mauser, as the gun came to be called, was an 11mm, single-shot bolt rifle that lacked nothing in the strength and formidability categories. The action involved a hefty steel bolt with a handle that projected straight out from the action, horizontally. When the bolt handle was moved upward, preparatory to opening the action, it was caught by a curved portion of the action body which cammed it slightly to the rear giving an extra boost to the extractor in pulling the case free of the chamber. The bolt

head was recessed and locking was effected by a long bar which fit within a slot on the right side of the receiver. A safety was mounted on the rear of the bolt. When the broad, paddle-shaped lever was turned to the left, the gun was ready to fire. All the way over to the right put the gun on safe.

The chosen cartridge, the 11.15x60R, was also designed by Peter Paul Mauser specifically for this rifle. Its 340-grain paper-patched bullet was backed with 77 grains of black powder. This gave the round a muzzle velocity of some 1,430 feet-per-second and a muzzle energy of 1,680 foot-pounds. The brass case was slightly bottlenecked and the beefy rim ensured very positive extraction.

The gun's barrel, which measured 30 inches, was rifled with four grooves with a 1 in 22 right-hand twist. Unquestionably, the gun was Wagnerian in concept, weighing in at over 10 pounds with an overall length of 48¾ inches. Everything on the piece was well-built, strong and extremely well thought out. Its bolt action was a considerable improvement over many

THE REAR SIGHT IS ACTUALLY A TAD OVER-BUILT. GRADUATED TO 1,600 YARDS, THE NARROW NOTCH MADE RAPID TARGET ACQUI-SITION SOMEWHAT OF A CHALLENGE.

FRONT SIGHTS ON 71/84 MAUSERS WERE DRIFT-ADJUSTABLE FOR WINDAGE. OUR GUN SHOT PRETTY MUCH RIGHT-ON AS-IS.

of the rotating blocks, lifting traps and falling blocks being used by other nations. It had another major advantage over these other single shots in that it, with just a little effort, could be turned into a repeater, which in 1884 it was.

By slightly reworking the stock and action configuration it was possible to amalgamate the original rifle with a Kropatschek-style tubular magazine originally developed in Austria. When the action was open and the cutoff lever pushed forward, a lifter/carrier

could be depressed and cartridges introduced into the under-barrel tube. Then, one simply worked the action though a complete cycle to chamber a round. Opening the action ejected the spent case and closing it put another cartridge up the spout. This could be repeated eight times until the mag was empty. If the soldier wanted to shoot the gun single shot and keep the remainder of his ammunition in reserve, he opened the bolt and moved the selector lever, which was located on the left rear of the receiver, backwards.

To fieldstrip the 71/84, first ensure the gun is unloaded. Now, loosen the large bolt-retaining screw, lift the retainer ring up and slide the bolt from the receiver. Next, pop off the long extractor on the left side of the bolt, rotate and remove the bolt head, and remove the short extractor. All quite simple.

Sights on the 71/84 consist of a blade front that is adjustable, via drift, for windage and a super-beefy ladder rear graduated to a fairly optimistic 1,600 meters. We found in shooting that the notch was a bit on the skimpy side and made rapid target acquisition at even 100 yards somewhat iffy, though aimed shots could be plonked into the target with little trouble.

Interestingly enough, I had been planning to do a Classic Test on the 71/84 for some time, so it was particularly fortuitous that Gibbs Rifle Company had just brought a slug of the things in from South America for the bargain price of $169.95 each. While they are not in mint condition like the ones that were imported in some quantity about 40 years ago, they are still pretty respectable and can make worthy shooters. Of course, our always reliable obsolete ammo source, The Old Western Scrounger, was able to come up with some new black powder 11mm Mauser fodder which fires a 340-grain unpatched lead bullet. Just the ticket.

Our evaluation piece from Gibbs was in pretty good shape. The bar-

TO PUT THE RIFLE ON SAFE, SIMPLY MOVE THE LEVER TO THE RIGHT. SWINGING IT ALL THE WAY TO THE LEFT READIES THE GUN FOR FIRING. THIS METHOD WOULD BE USED IN OTHER LATER MAUSERS.

IF ONE WANTED TO FIRE THE 71/84 SINGLE SHOT, THE CUT-OFF LEVER COULD BE ACTIVATED. THIS KEPT THE FOLLOWER FROM PICKING UP ROUNDS FROM THE MAGAZINE.

rel, bands, triggerguard and other appropriate parts exhibited about 90 percent of their original blue and bright metal parts. The parts were, for the most part, pretty blemish-free, with the exception of the bolt, which had turned slightly brown. The serial number on the bolt did not match that of the gun, but it functioned just fine. The full-length walnut stock, while dented and gouged here and there, was sound overall, and the royal cipher storekeeper's marks could be seen plainly and deeply stamped into the butt.

The bore was pristine and the mechanics just fine, including a 4½-pound, double-stage, military-style trigger pull that, while not particularly onerous, was not conducive to match-grade accuracy. Still, we managed some pretty good groups at 100 and 50 yards, though we found that the spreads were improved mightily when the bore was swabbed out after each shot. Remember, our new ammo was not paper-patched as was the original and this could make some difference.

The gun functioned perfectly, exhibited little recoil and operated very well as a repeater. Cases were lifted from the magazine, chambered and ejected very efficiently. All in all, a pretty neat package. There is talk of allowing these guns to be used in the long-range big-bore Cowboy Action shooting events. My guess is that with a little gun/load tuning they could perform extremely well, and the round's ballistics is right there in the .45-70 range …. probably the most popular chambering for these matches.

I think the last time I fired a Model 71 or 71/84 Mauser was at least 45 years ago (I was very young, you understand), and the joy of popping the guns off using very reliable original ammo is something that stayed with me. This reacquaintance with my old friend has been long overdue.

Fieldstripping

To fieldstrip the 71/84, first ensure the gun is unloaded. (1) Next, open the bolt and loosen the retaining screw. (2) Lift the retaining washer and remove the bolt. (3) Pop off the long extractor on the side of the bolt. (4) Rotate and remove the bolt head. (5) Remove the short extractor.

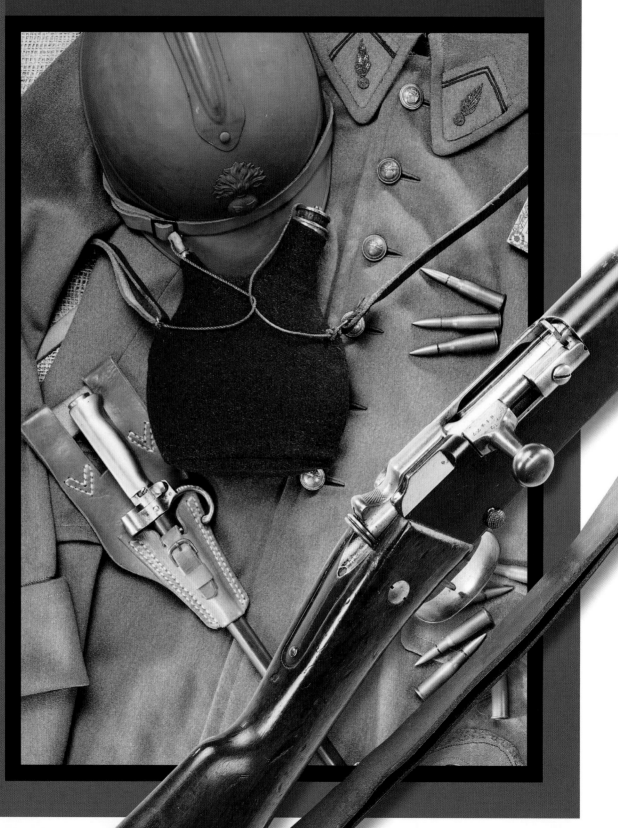

CLASSIC TEST

*Though awkward by modern
standards, this revolutionary arm was
the secret weapon of its day.*

It was ungainly; a Frankenstein-like put-together of older firearms components. In practically no time it would be eclipsed by far more sophisticated designs…but for one brief moment, this unlikely piece of armament was the most coveted secret weapon of its day.

The French Fusile Modele 1886, better known as the "Lebel," was the first smokeless powder military longarm to be fielded by any army. Arms experts printed wild speculations concerning the effectiveness of the gun's 8mm round: "According to French accounts, the powder is both smokeless and noiseless. If this were the case, no doubt it would produce changes in the mode of fighting and surprise would be greatly facilitated. Last year, however, experiments were conducted at the German Artillery School and at the Manouevres with an almost

identical powder, the results of which proved that the advantages of the French powder were greatly exaggerated." While the above report from the 1890 edition of *Armies of Europe* is largely true, a certain amount of sour grapes is discernible. The new French Poudre B was a revolutionary step forward in military small arms development, and one emulated by most of the world's major powers.

In 1885, after considerable experimentation, researchers Monsieur Vielle and Captain Desalaux came up with a practical smokeless powder which offered considerable velocity with manageable pressures and little fouling, and French authorities immediately began developing a new round and rifle to accommodate it.

The chosen cartridge had a tapered, rimmed bottleneck case and a nickel-jacketed 216-grain, round-nosed 8mm bullet which left the muzzle at a then-astounding velocity of 2,350 fps. The rifle, though, was not anywhere near as revolutionary as the round, being basically an amalgam of the older French service arms.

In 1878 the French equipped their marines

THE MODEL 1886 LEBEL WAS A LONG, UNGAINLY ARM WHOSE LOOKS BELIED ITS EFFECTIVENESS. IT WAS ONE OF THE PRIMARY RIFLES OF WORLD WAR I AND WAS VERY POPULAR WITH THE FRENCH "POILU."

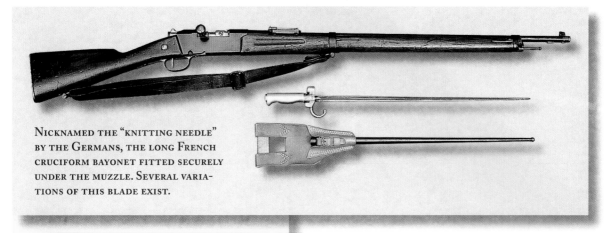

Nicknamed the "knitting needle" by the Germans, the long French cruciform bayonet fitted securely under the muzzle. Several variations of this blade exist.

Ammunition is loaded into the Lebel's tubular magazine one round at a time. The round-nose bullet employed by the Balle M cartridge eliminated the possibility of an accidental nose-to-tail discharge.

Like most military arms of the period, the '86 Lebel was equipped with a cutoff for single shots. The mechanism is activated by a side-mounted button that locks and unlocks the magazine follower.

The front sight involved a wide blade that incorporated a small notch at the rear which was used as a primitive "night sight."

The Lebel rear sight was graduated to 2,400 meters. Flipping the ladder forward completely exposed the battle sight.

with a version of the Austrian Kropatschek bolt-action repeater—an 11mm black powder arm featuring a tubular, under-barrel magazine. Rounds were loaded into the magazine one behind the other against a spring-loaded metal plunger. A floorplate, hinged at the rear, dropped down when the bolt was closed, ready to receive a cartridge. When the bolt was opened and a case ejected, the follower snapped up, placing a round in chambering position.

French authorities determined that this action, though a tad archaic, would be acceptable for the new cartridge. The Fusile Modele 1886 was also called the M86 Lebel after its designer Colonel Lebel, though there was little new in it, the gun being little more than a modification of the Modele 1878 Fusile de Marine with an older-style Gras-type bolt and a modification of front-locking lugs to accommodate Poudre B's higher pressures.

The Lebel had a slab-sided receiver, necessitating the use of a two-piece stock. It measured 51 inches overall, weighed 9½ pounds and had a 31½-inch barrel. The magazine held eight rounds, with a round in the carrier and one in the chamber for a 10-shot capacity. Balle M's round-nosed bullet eliminated the possibility of accidentally discharging the nose-to-tail cartridges in the magazine.

Further tests and use in the field pointed up a few weaknesses in the arm. In 1893 the bolt head was modified to allow gas to be safely vented should a primer be pierced, and the receiver was strengthened slightly to accommodate the new, heavier pressures. This altered arm was designated, appropriately enough, the

Fusile Modele 86/93. It is this version most often encountered by modern collectors.

The sights of the M86 experienced several modifications during the rifle's life span. The rear ladder-type sight was initially graduated to 2,000 meters, though with the development of new loads, this was eventually upped to 2,400 meters. The ladder could be rotated completely forward exposing a 250-meter battle sight notch. Early front sight blades incorporated a depression at the rear which contained a small amount of radium for night use.

Balle D was brought into service in 1898 incorporating a 197-grain, pointed bullet which dramatically increased the effective range. An O-ring crimp surrounding the primer eliminated the possibility of chain firing. In 1932 the hotter Balle N was developed for machine guns, and many M86 rifles were reproved for use with this round. Guns safe for use with Balle N are stamped with a large "N" on top of their barrels and receivers. Rifles without this designation are unsafe to shoot with late French service ammunition.

Our evaluation rifle was an M86/93 that had been proved for Balle N, so the ammo used was some 1940s vintage French issue fodder. Some commercial Remington ammunition was produced years ago and ammo can be made by forming .348 Winchester brass. Neither of these loads features the O-ring crimp, however, and must be loaded single shot. Never stoke an '86 Lebel magazine with any of this ammo!

The trigger had a long two-stage pull that broke at about 5 pounds. The gun functioned perfectly, with the rounds feeding flawlessly from the tube. Unfortunately the same cannot be said for the ammo which did give us a hang-fire or two which probably affected the groups, which ran about 6 inches at 100 yards. Recoil, by the way, was relatively light, as one might expect in a 9½-pound rifle. Sights were adequate, and we were even able to hit a 200-yard gong pretty regularly using the battle sight.

Certainly, the '86 was obsolete almost as soon as it came out, but with proper ammunition it can still provide a lot of good sport.

Removing the Bolt

TO REMOVE THE LEBEL'S BOLT, FIRST ENSURE THE GUN IS UNLOADED. (1) NOW, REMOVE THE SCREW THAT JOINS THE BOLT HEAD AND BOLT TOGETHER. (2,3) ROTATE THE BOLT HEAD TO THE RIGHT UNTIL IT SEPARATES FROM THE BOLT. (4,5) REMOVE THE BOLT HEAD AND BODY FROM THE RECEIVER.

Classic Military Rifles
British Long Lee-Enfield

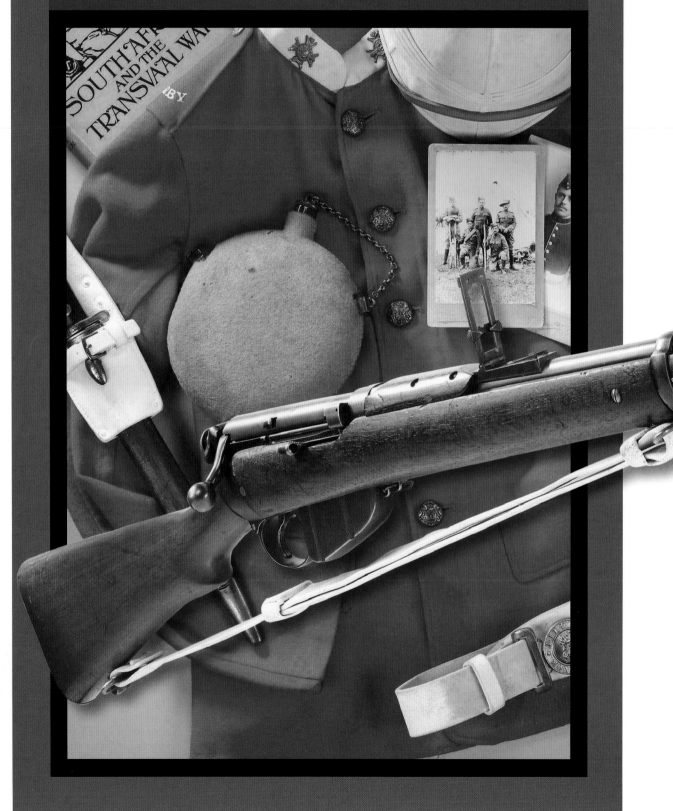

*This repeater was the first
of a noble line of fine military rifles.*

I know the whole question of "Empire" has come up for criticism since the 1920s, but for one such as myself, steeped in the writings of Rider Haggard, Winston Churchill, and Richard Harding Davis, it holds considerable fascination. There is no question that many Victorian empire builders were colorful, larger-than-life characters who risked personal fortune—even their lives—to make sure that much of the globe remained under British influence.

No matter how engaging one's personality, there is a limit to what he can do without force of arms. England was particularly blessed in the latter part of the 19th century with a disciplined military armed with some of the finest arms available at the time. Topmost among them was the Long Lee-Enfield.

The Lee-Enfield had something of an American connection. James Paris Lee was a naturalized U.S. citizen whose parents had emigrated from Scotland 1835. Originally a watchmaker, Lee was fascinated by firearms and eventually moved to Wisconsin, where he took up gun design full time.

Lee perfected the box magazine and submitted a bolt-action repeater for evaluation by both the United States Army and Navy. This "Remington-Lee" drew the attention of the British War Department, which tested a rifle chambered for drawn brass .577-450 versions of the British service cartridge, fitted with Martini-Henry barrels.

The gun proved to be reliable and trials continued through the 1880s with modified Remington-Lees, and more standard versions chambered for .45-70 and .43 Spanish.

Though the British had been considering adopting a .402 service round, they took notice

THE LONG LEE-ENFIELD'S ACTION IS PRETTY MUCH THE SAME AS THAT USED ON THE EARLIER LEE-METFORD. THE SAFETY LEVER MOUNTED ON THE COCKING PIECE WAS VERY EASY TO USE. LIKE MANY MILITARY ARMS OF THE PERIOD, THE LONG LEE-ENFIELD INCORPORATED A SHEET METAL BOLT COVER.

THE CARTRIDGES WERE INTENDED TO BE LOADED SINGLY INTO THE BOX MAGAZINE THROUGH THE TOP OF THE ACTION. A MAGAZINE CUT-OFF WAS PROVIDED TO ALLOW THE RIFLE TO BE FIRED SINGLE SHOT.

THE BOX MAGAZINE COULD BE REMOVED TO HANG FREE BY A LOOP BENEATH THE RIFLE. BRITISH MILITARY PLANNERS ORIGINALLY INTENDED THAT A SOLDIER WOULD CARRY A SPARE MAGAZINE FOR RAPID FIRE SITUATIONS.

DIAL OR MUSKETRY SIGHTS GRADUATED TO 2,800 YARDS ALLOWED MEN TO FIRE MASSED VOLLEYS AT LONG RANGE. THESE WERE SEEN ON THE EARLY MARK III SMLE'S, BUT WERE ELIMINATED DURING WORLD WAR I, ONLY TO REAPPEAR BRIEFLY ON THE SEMI-EXPERIMENTAL MARK V SMLE.

of Swiss .303 smallbore experiments and settled on that caliber. The Lee system mated to a seven-groove barrel designed by William E. Metford and chambered in .303 Swiss Rubin.

In December of 1888, the Magazine Lee-Metford Rifle, Mark I, was officially accepted into British service. The .303 round had a drawn brass case and a 215-grain cupro-nickel-jacketed round-nose bullet backed by 71½ grains of blackpowder in pellet form.

Her Majesty's first general-issue repeating service rifle was a good-looking, rugged arm. Featuring a bolt action, it had an eight-shot box magazine which protruded in front of the triggerguard. While it could be removed, this was not standard practice, as it was actually linked to the gun and rounds were to be loaded into the rifle through the top of the action. In addition, the magazine was equipped with a cut-off that allowed the gun to be fired as a single shot—the reasoning being that the rounds in the magazine should be kept in reserve.

The bolt was not as strong as some Mauser designs, but was perfectly adequate for the pressures developed by the .303 service round. The fact that it cocked on closing made it easy to operate rapidly. Locking was achieved by means of a lug and solid rib on the bolt. The former engaged a recess in the receiver, the latter was secured against a shoulder. The bolt head was a separate piece threaded on to the bolt body.

As well as an elegant rear ladder sight graduated to 1,900 yards, the Lee-Metford was equipped with a dial sight mounted on the right side of the forestock. When employed properly, it enabled the soldier to fire for effect at ranges up to 3,500 yards!

The rifle's overall length was 49½ inches with a 30-inch barrel. The stock was full length and consisted of a separate fore-end and butt which were attached to a socket on the receiver.

In 1892 sights were regraduated and the safety catch eliminated. A year later the magazine capacity was increased to 10 and the bolt improved. In 1895 a safety catch was placed on the rear of the cocking piece.

Lee-Metford also manufactured carbines.

While they retained the same mechanics as the infantry rifle, the weapons were shortened considerably for mounted use. In addition, the sight was altered and the bolt knob flattened.

In 1886 the French had adopted smokeless powder for their Lebel rifle and British planners realized it was imperative that they keep pace with modern developments.

On November 3, 1891, Britain adopted its first smokeless load, the Cartridge, S.A., Ball .303 Cordite, Mark I. The round

REMOVING THE LEE'S BOLT IS AS SIMPLE AS PULLING THE BOLT TO THE REAR, SNAPPING THE BOLT HEAD STUD FREE FROM ITS CHANNEL ON THE RECEIVER AND WITHDRAWING IT FROM THE RECEIVER.

used a drawn brass case and 215-grain bullet, with a charge of 31 grains (60 strands) of Cordite, a spaghetti-like propellant made from nitroglycerine, guncotton and mineral jelly. Cordite was relatively smoke-free and upped the muzzle velocity from 1,850 to 1,970 fps. Unfortunately, it burned much hotter than blackpowder and caused severe erosion in the Metford rifling.

Designers quickly came up with a simple solution. They replaced the older barrels with ones rifled with five deep angular grooves, which were less affected by the new propellant. Termed "Enfield" rifling after the Royal Ordnance Factory where the system was developed, the stage was set for one of the most important military arms ever developed: the Lee-Enfield. The first Lee-Enfield was approved Nov. 11, 1895.

The .303 cartridge itself had undergone some changes as well, and in 1893 the Boxer primer was replaced with a Berdan design.

From the outside, the Long Lee-Enfield was virtually indistinguishable from the Metfords, even down to the sight graduations. It was with this gun, as well as its modification, the Mk I (which eliminated the cleaning rod), that the British fought the Boers in 1899. In battle the Lee-Enfield acquitted itself quite well against

the Boer Mausers.

Some sighting difficulties—along with the Enfield's inability to be charged rapidly with clips—did cause problems. At the Battle of Spion Kop in January, 1900 this became all too evident. "A cyclone of death had smitten the summit," recounted the editors of *With the Flag to Pretoria*. "No words can describe the appalling uproar...the British soldier...was at a grave disadvantage, for the rifle with which he was armed was awkward to load lying down; the Boer weapon with its clip holding five cartridges could be charged easily..."

Lessons of the Boer War were taken to heart by authorities, and plans were set in motion to design a rifle that could be charger loaded, and would be of such length that it could be used by both infantry and cavalry. In 1902 the famed Short Magazine Lee-Enfield was approved.

My Long-Lee Enfield is a basic Mk I issue rifle, manufactured by L.S.A. in 1896. It retains all standard appurtenances, including the long-range dial sight, ramrod channel beneath the barrel, bolt cover, cocking-piece-mounted safety and unit markings on the buttplate tang.

For testing I used Winchester 174-grain FMJ .303 ammo. At 100 yards rested groups ran a monotonous 1½ to 2 inches. As the gun hefts some 9 pounds 4 ounces, recoil was anything but punishing, and I was able to work the action and fire 10 rounds in about as many seconds. The trigger pull was a crisp 7½ pounds—more than adequate for military.

The Long Lee was a superb weapon—one of the best of its time. It provided the basis for an even better arm, the SMLE, and in that gun really rests the lasting legacy of the British Long Lee-Enfield.

*To many collectors,
this superbly made bolt-action
military rifle represents the
crown jewel of all Model 98 variants.*

I can't recall the exact date in the mid-1950s, but I can remember what happened like it was last week. There, on a table at an Ohio gun show, was this beautiful rifle. It talked to me, and I listened despite my father's warning that there was no sense in buying some "foreign" rifle that shot ammo no one could get. But who ever said gun deals have to make sense?

At the time I had no clue that there was any difference in status between that pristine Model 1909 Argentine Mauser still in cosmoline and any other garden-variety surplus rifle. Yes, I knew what Mausers were, but I couldn't have discussed the differences among them. All I knew was that I wanted that rifle and was willing to put down the 40 silver dollars it took to walk away with it. I used silver dollars

THE HEART OF THE MODEL 1909 ARGENTINE IS ITS LARGE-RING MAUSER ACTION. THIS CLASSIC MODEL 98 VARIANT EXHIBITS FIT, FINISH AND WORKMANSHIP THAT WOULD BE PROHIBITIVELY EXPENSIVE TO DUPLICATE ON A MODERN PRODUCTION SPORTER.

for all gun purchases during that era, and 40 of them was a healthy price for a surplus Mauser. In fact, it was more than the rifle was probably worth, but the Mauser was in considerably better condition than most surplus rifles available during those years. Fortunately, the purchase also included a bag of corrosive military ammo. About half of the cartridges failed to fire despite fairly deep firing-pin indentations on the primer. But somehow that didn't really matter. The rifle shot well, looked great and functioned like a Swiss watch.

Because 7.65 Argentine ammo was generally unavailable at the time, I was forced to begin reloading centerfire rifle ammo and it wasn't long before I took simple reloading of Norma cases to another level. I purchased a form/trim die from RCBS and began converting .30-06 cases into 7.65x53mm brass—something that I continue to do to this day.

As full-length Model 1909 Argentine Mausers go, this particular specimen is typical of those imported during the 1950s, complete

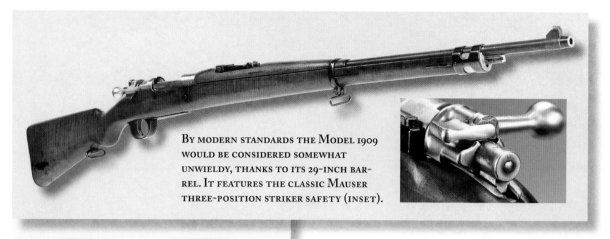

By modern standards the Model 1909 would be considered somewhat unwieldy, thanks to its 29-inch barrel. It features the classic Mauser three-position striker safety (inset).

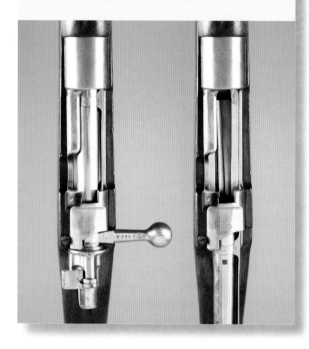

Open and shut: The Model 1909 Argentine feeds from a five-round box magazine. Countless straight bolts were bent down to produce "scope-friendly" sporters. Unlike other Mausers of the time, the bolt release continues over the top of the receiver bridge.

with the Argentine crest ground off the top of the receiver ring. The crests were removed after surplus rifles, bearing the Argentine liberty cap and sun motif, wound up in the hands of Chaco rebels in Paraguay in the 1930s.

In the aftermath of the devastating War of the Triple Alliance fought with Argentina, Uruguay and Brazil allied against Paraguay between 1865 and 1870, the Argentine army was transformed into a professional military force. By 1890 the Argentines abandoned their

single-shot Remington rolling blocks in favor of the new 1891 Mauser bolt-action repeaters. In 1909 Argentina purchased a commercial version of Germany's sturdy Gehwehr 98 military rifle manufactured by the Deutsche Waffen und Munitionsfabriken in Berlin. The new rifles were designated the Mauser Modelo Argentino 1909 (Argentine Mauser Model 1909) and marked with the Argentine national crest on the receiver ring. Some were marked Ejercito Argentino (Argentine army) on the side rail or ring. The Model 1909 differed from its German prototype with the addition of a tangent rear sight, hinged magazine floorplate, and a modified upper hand guard. The Argentines also added an auxiliary bayonet lug attached over the rifle's original lug to allow use of the Model 1891 bayonet.

The 7.65mm Argentine cartridge predates any rifles Argentina ever had chambered for it. Technically, it is the 7.65x53mm Mauser cartridge (or 7.65x53mm Belgian Mauser) introduced in the Model 1889 Belgian Mauser rifle. Over the years, a number of other countries adopted the round for military purposes including Bolivia, Colombia, Ecuador, Peru and Turkey. Military rifles to shoot it were made primarily in Germany as export rifles, but a "clone" factory was established in Argentina, and as many as 85,000 Argentine Mausers were made locally.

My rifle was made by the Deutsche Waffen und Munitionsfabriken (DWM), one of the better-known German Mauser manufacturers at the time. It has always fascinated me why the export rifles made for other countries were always so much better made than the rifles Germany made for itself. But that's another story.

Model 1909s generally came in two configurations: the full-length rifle and the carbine. Carbine versions were manufactured for cavalry and in a version intended for mountain troops. A special sniper model was issued with a turned down bolt and German-made telescopic scope and mounts.

I have owned both carbine and standard rifle versions and prefer the full-length rifle, which weighs a nominal 9.25 pounds. It has a five-round magazine capacity and sports a 29-inch barrel with .301 bore and .311 groove diameters. The four-groove rifling has a right-hand twist rate of one turn in 9.8 inches. Although the military bullets were .313 of an inch in diameter, the Argentine Mausers shoot .311 and .312 bullets just fine.

There were two primary military loadings for the cartridge. One sent a 211-grain bullet out of the barrel at a nominal 2,132 fps while the latter loading shot a 185-grain bullet at 2,467 fps. This is just shy of the modern .308 Winchester cartridge in performance, and it's easy (and safe) to duplicate .308 performance in the Model 1909. (However, it's not a good idea to shoot the faster loads in the earlier '91 Argentines.) Norma factory loads for the 7.65x53mm include a 150-grain bullet at 2,920 fps and a 180-grain bullet at 2,590 fps.

Sights on the 1909 Argentine are classic Mauser tangent propositions with an inverted-"V" front post and a "V"-notched rear sight that is calibrated to a "harassing fire" range of 2,000 meters, with a bottom setting for a 300-meter battle sight. This means that most unaltered rifles shoot roughly four inches high at 100 yards. With judicious handloading, however, you can create loads that will shoot right to the point of aim at 100 yards—pretty handy for general use.

Accuracy? On a good day with the open military sights I can put five shots into about a 1¼-inch cluster at 100 yards.

Fit and finish of the metal parts are beyond mere imagination. Few custom rifles these days are better finished, both internally and

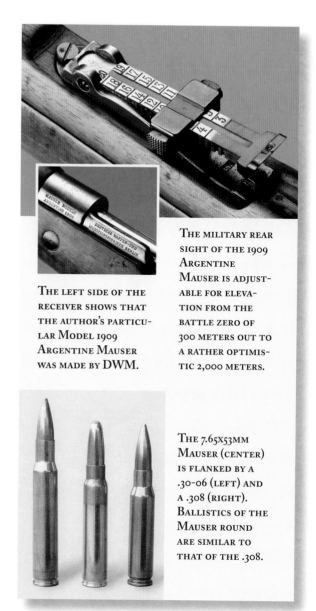

THE LEFT SIDE OF THE RECEIVER SHOWS THAT THE AUTHOR'S PARTICULAR MODEL 1909 ARGENTINE MAUSER WAS MADE BY DWM.

THE MILITARY REAR SIGHT OF THE 1909 ARGENTINE MAUSER IS ADJUSTABLE FOR ELEVATION FROM THE BATTLE ZERO OF 300 METERS OUT TO A RATHER OPTIMISTIC 2,000 METERS.

THE 7.65X53MM MAUSER (CENTER) IS FLANKED BY A .30-06 (LEFT) AND A .308 (RIGHT). BALLISTICS OF THE MAUSER ROUND ARE SIMILAR TO THAT OF THE .308.

externally. In fact, the 1909 Argentine action became one of the favorites of custom riflemakers for decades. This was because it was not only extremely strong but also dimensionally correct and consistent.

I have owned literally hundreds of surplus Mausers from countries around the world. But somehow, none has quite the same place in my heart as my first Argentine Model 1909. It helped launch my lifelong commitment to the shooting sports. When I have this rifle in my hands, all is right with the world.

Mark III Short Magazine Lee-Enfield

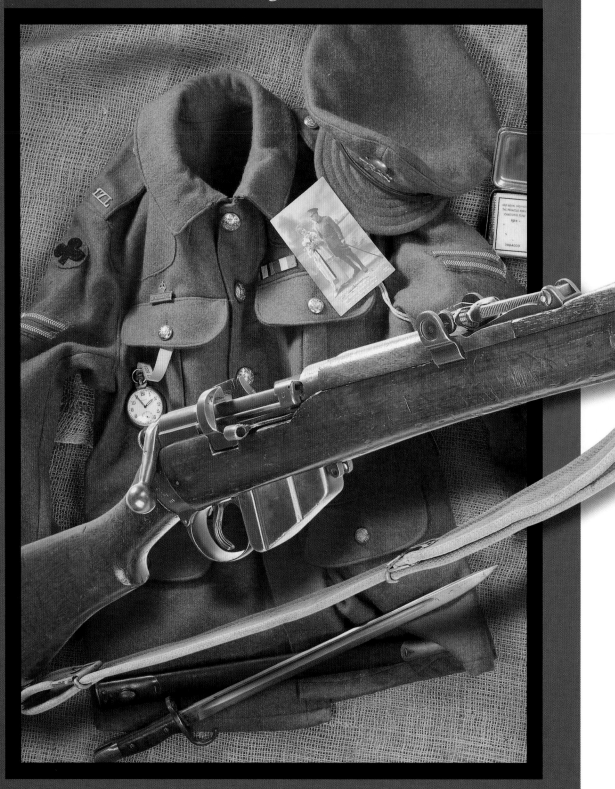

This gun just may be the best military bolt-action rifle ever issued.

After shooting one for over 40 years, the Mark III Short Magazine Lee-Enfield (SMLE) is my favorite-ever bolt-action military rifle. While this may sound rather disingenuous on my part, I will try, in these next few pages, to justify my blatant prejudice.

Actually the Mark III, while produced in huge numbers during and between the world wars, was neither the first nor the last of its line. In 1888, after considerable trial and testing, the British government adopted the Magazine Lee-Metford Rifle, Mark I, a 49½-inch bolt-action repeating rifle firing a .303 caliber blackpowder cartridge based on a Swiss design.

With the introduction of the French smokeless powder 8mm Lebel round in 1886, however, nations all over the globe began redesigning arms and cartridges to handle the new propel-

THE MARK III ENFIELD WAS JUST AS RUGGED AS IT LOOKED. IT WAS AMONG THE PREEMINENT BATTLE RIFLES OF THE FIRST WORLD WAR.

lents. The British were no exception, and in 1891 they adopted a .303 with a 215-grain bullet propelled by 31 grains of Cordite, a spaghetti-like material made from nitroglycerine, guncotton and mineral jelly.

Unfortunately this hot new load was not well suited to the Metford rifling and reports of serious bore erosion began to filter back from the field. Accordingly, experts set to work to modify the Lee's rifling to better handle the new round. What emerged was a more angular, deeper five-groove rifling that would not be affected by the new propellant, termed "Enfield" rifling because it was developed at the Royal Ordnance Factory at that location, it heralded the beginning of a firearms legend—the Lee-Enfield.

Initially the Lee-Enfield (and Lee-Metfords, for that matter) were produced in long barrelled infantry versions and short cavalry carbines. Authorities eventually decided that it would be more prudent logistically and cost-wise to have one gun that could suit both purposes.

EARLY MARK IIIs, LIKE
THEIR PREDECESSORS,
HAD SLIDING CUTOFFS
TO ALLOW THE GUN TO
BE FIRED SINGLE SHOT
WHILE TEN ROUNDS
WERE HELD IN THE
MAGAZINE AS RESERVE.
THIS FEATURE WAS
ABANDONED ALONG
WITH THE DIAL SIGHT
TO SIMPLIFY MANUFAC-
TURE DURING WORLD
WAR I.

After extensive testing, the Mk I Short Magazine Lee-Enfield was approved just prior to Christmas, 1902. This gun was a handy 44¼ inches overall, with an Enfield rifled barrel of just slightly over 25 inches. It was stocked to the end of the muzzle and had a generous nose

cap that formed a pair of large "wings" to protect the front sight.

The rear ladder sight was graduated to 2,000 yards, the slide being released by a pair of buttons on either side. Long-range "volley-fire" or "dial" sights, marked to 2,800 yards were inlet into the left side of the stock.

The bolt head was fitted with a guide, which permitted the use of a five-round stripper clip or "charger." Now ten rounds could be loaded into the magazine in just seconds.

January 1907 saw the debut of the subject of this article, the Mark III SMLE—a gun that was to perform yeoman service in two world wars as well as campaigns in India and other remote parts of the world. Undoubtedly one of the most famous rifles ever made, the Mark III was a reliable, sturdy arm that operated admirably in extreme conditions.

Externally it resembled the Mark I with the major difference being the addition of a charger bridge across the receiver. This robust design was a considerable improvement over the bolt-end guide and one that was greatly appreciated by the soldiers to whom the rifle was issued.

THE MARK III COULD BE LOADED EASI-
LY VIA FIVE-ROUND CLIPS. CARTRIDGES
HAD TO BE LOADED IN THE PROPER
OVERLAPPING MANNER OR THEY
WOULDN'T FEED PROPERLY.

THE MARK III'S SAFETY
INVOLVED A SMALL LEVER
ON THE LEFT SIDE OF THE
RECEIVER THAT COULD BE
EASILY FLICKED OFF WITH
THE THUMB. THERE WAS
ALSO A HALF-COCK NOTCH
ON THE STRIKER.

TO REMOVE THE MARK III'S BOLT, SIMPLY PULL UP AND
UNLOCK THE BOLT RELEASE LEVER AND PULL THE BOLT
ASSEMBLY FREE OF THE ACTION.

Experiments were also being conducted to improve the .303 Cordite cartridge which had scarcely changed since its introduction. Various bullet weights and types were tested and in 1907 the Mark VII load made its debut. It had a pointed cupro-nickel-jacketed bullet of 174 grains, with a 37-grain charge of MDT. This round would remain basically unmodified up to the demise of the Lee-Enfield in the service.

The Mark III was the primary longarm Britain carried into World War I. As the conflict dragged on and more and more rifles were urgently needed at the front, manufacturing shortcuts were adopted. These included the elimination of the gun's sliding cartridge cutoff, dial sights, rear sight wind gauge and brass stock identification discs. Most of the features were superfluities anyway, and their omission did little to affect the Mark III's (now termed Mk III) effectiveness in the field.

The gun won nothing but accolades from its users and respect from its adversaries. At the Battle of Mons, for instance, the British were firing their Enfields so rapidly and with such great effect that the Germans thought they were facing massed machine guns.

Mark IIIs continued to be manufactured through World War II, mainly by the Australians, who generally carried it in favor of the British general service No. 4 Mk I.

Our evaluation rifle was an old warhorse I had in my collection. It is a stock Mk III, retaining all of the rifle's early issue features. Condition was quite good and the bore excellent, though there is no question that this customer has seen some serious service.

The trigger, while stagey, came in at just over five pounds. Chosen ammo was Winchester 174-grain FMJ and PMC 180-grain SP.

The gun was fired from a rest and offhand at 100 yards. Loading with the clips was a snap, and we experienced nary a feeding or shooting malfunction throughout the evaluation. Recoil, even with the bare, naked brass buttplate was not prohibitive, and as per the Tommy of 1914, we were able to rip off rapid-fire shots at the rate of about one every second and a half.

NOT INTENDED TO BE ROUTINELY REMOVED FROM THE RIFLE, THE SHEET STEEL MAGAZINE COULD BE RELEASED VIA A SMALL LEVER ON THE INSIDE, FORWARD PORTION OF THE TRIGGERGUARD.

SIGHTS INVOLVED A VERY SOPHISTICATED LADDER REAR, GRADUATED TO 2,000 YARDS, AND BLADE FRONT SURROUNDED BY TWO STURDY "WINGS."

EARLY LEE-ENFIELDS WERE FITTED WITH VOLLEY-FIRE SIGHTS ON THE LEFT SIDE OF THE STOCK (ABOVE AND LEFT)—SORT OF A POOR MAN'S ARTILLERY. WHEN PROPERLY ADJUSTED THEY COULD BE USED FOR INDIRECT FIRE.

Accuracy was pretty darned good, with groups running in the 3-inch category with both brands of ammo. While we didn't take the gun and drag it around in the mud or hose it down to see how it would work under adverse, trench-style conditions, I will take the vets' words for it that it was probably the most reliable battle rifle to come out of the Great War. It's still my favorite, and I really can't see anything overtaking it, in my estimation at least, in the foreseeable future.

Winchester Russian Model 1895

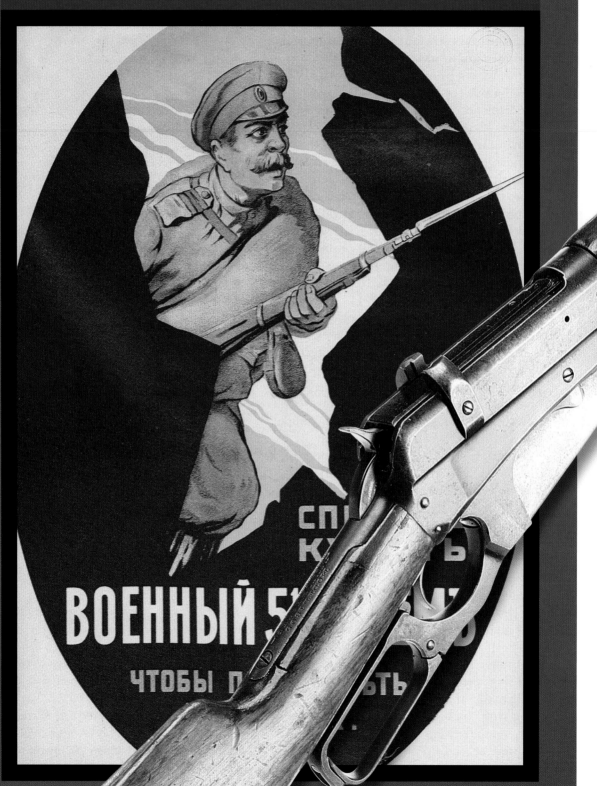

Ordered as an emergency arm in World War One,
This lever gun is still a good shooter.

In the late summer of 1914, Paris was doomed, or so it seemed. The German Army was within sight of the eternal city, and only a miracle could save her from the same humiliation she had endured at the hands of conquering Germans in 1871. And then the "Miracle of the Marne" occurred. One and a half million Russians attacked at Tannenberg in the east, drawing away valuable resources and men from the German offensive. Paris was saved. Stalemate settled in on the Western front. The Great War would not be over anytime soon.

Nearly half of the Russian infantry that attacked at Tannenberg went into battle completely unarmed! Like the Chinese who over-ran the Chosin Reservoir in Korea some 35 years later, most of the 2nd and 3rd waves of Russian infantry advanced using the firearms dropped by their fallen comrades. Russia was woefully unprepared to supply an army in the field with proper equipment and arms. The Russian minister of war, Alexei Polivanov, estimated that in 1915 he had nearly one million unarmed soldiers. "Rifles," he wrote, "were more precious than gold."

Immediately contracts were executed with foreign arms manufactures for rifles and muni-

tions. Remington Arms and Westinghouse were given orders for one million Russian service rifles, the Model 1891 Mosin-Nagant. The Winchester Repeating Arms Company of New Haven, Connecticut, received a contract to supply the Czar's army with 300,000 rifles based on the John Browning-designed Winchester M-1895 lever-action. Known as the Winchester Model 95 "Russian Musket," these arms comprised nearly 75 percent of all the Model 1895s manufactured between 1896 (the year of introduction) and 1931 when production ceased.

The Winchester Model 1895 Lever Action (Winchester also introduced a straight-pull, bolt-action rifle in 1895) was John Browning's response to the development of high-powered smokeless rifle cartridges. Ballistic developments that followed the introduction of smokeless powder in the late 1880s brought with them changes in bullet design. With small caliber, high-velocity cartridges, bullet aerodynamics became a focus of attention. The introduction of cartridges with pointed spitzer bullets could in theory render most lever actions of the day obsolete and dangerous to carry. All lever guns of the period were fed from a tubular magazine.

THE WINCHESTER RUSSIAN MODEL 1895 RIFLE LOOKS PRETTY MUCH LIKE THAT COMPANY'S STANDARD MUSKET, WITH THE ADDITION OF A CLIP GUIDE MOUNTED ATOP THE RECEIVER.

AS WE WERE NOT ABLE TO LOCATE A PROPER MOSIN-NAGANT STRIPPER CLIP, ROUNDS HAD TO BE PRESSED INTO THE BOX MAGAZINE ONE AT A TIME.

The tendency for the pointed nose of one round to pierce the primer of another round and discharge was very real if the gun was dropped. The genius of Browning's design was that his lever-action rifle was fed from an internal box magazine, giving the shooter an advantage in speed and retention of sight-picture that his bolt-action competitor did not have.

Originally offered in .30 U.S. (.30-40 Krag), .38-72 WCF and .40-72 WCF, the Winchester 1895 was eventually chambered in .30-03, .30-06, .303, .35 WCF and .405 WCF, a favorite chambering of President Theodore Roosevelt, who took 95s on his African Safari of 1910 and down the Brazilian River of Doubt in 1913.

The Russian Model 1895, which was adopted in 1915, had its design roots in a rifle that had been made some 15 years before and used in the Philippine Campaign. Faced with a similar shortage of rifles when the American war with Spain broke out in April of 1898, the American secretary of war, Russell Alger, ordered 10,000 Winchester Model 1895 lever-action muskets.

The first delivery took place while Spanish diplomats were negotiating an end to the war. The musket that Winchester produced for the U.S. in 1898 and for the Russians in 1915 was a full-stocked rifle with a 28-inch barrel and a Winchester blade bayonet.

In September of 1899, 100 of the U.S. Winchester 1895 muskets were issued to the 33rd U.S. Volunteer Infantry for field trials and evaluation in the Philippine Islands, an active theater of combat until 1903. On Christmas Day 1900, Major General Arthur MacArthur, commanding the U.S. Army in the Philippines (and the father of the future Army General Douglas MacArthur) cabled the Adjutant General in Washington that the standard service Krag rifle was "generally considered superior and much preferred" to the 1895 Winchester. He cited difficulty with loading as one of the prime reasons the rifle did not pass muster. The Chief of Ordnance in 1901 wrote, "These arms are not suited for the United States service." In 1906 the Army commercially disposed of all 10,000, with most ending up in the service of military units in the Caribbean and Central America.

Having been damned with less than even faint praise, it would seem that the curtain had been drawn on any future military sales of a lever-action Winchester. Yet when procurement agents for the Russian Defense Ministry began searching the globe for rifles in 1915, Winchester quickly offered the 1895 musket as a substitute standard to the M1891 Mosin-Nagant. The Russian 95 was chambered in the standard Russian service caliber of 7.62 mm. (Although by 1916, standard anythings were considered a great rarity among Russian troops. One regiment had no less than 10 different rifle calibers represented within its ranks.) The 7.62x54R round, which was originally designated for the Mosin-Nagant rifle, had a

FUNCTIONING OF OUR EVALUATION PIECE WAS FLAWLESS, WITH CHAMBERING AND EJECTION VERY POSITIVE. RECOIL WAS A TAD ON THE STOUT SIDE.

SIGHTS ON THE WINCHESTER RUSSIAN MODEL 1895 INVOLVE A MILITARY-STYLE LADDER REAR GRADUATED TO 3,200 YARDS AND A BLADE FRONT. A LUG FOR A BLADE BAYONET IS SITUATED ON THE BOTTOM OF THE FRONT BARREL BAND.

rimmed, tapered case. The original 210-grain round-nosed bullet lacked accuracy and puissance. Fortunately, the development by the Germans of the spitzer bullet gave the round a new lease on life, and in 1909 an improved "L" round was adopted. With a 150-grain bullet and adjusted powder charge, the ballistics of the cartridge were boosted to almost 2,900 fps.

The blade bayonet was visually identical to the US 1895 model but just different enough to prevent interchangeability. Stripper clip guides were mounted on the receiver to allow rapid loading of the five cartridges. Markings consist of the Russian acceptance cartouche on the receiver breech and 7.62, denoting the correct caliber.

A total of 300,000 Model 95 Muskets were delivered to the Russians in 1915 and 1916.

The sights on the Russian Model 1895

consist of a rear ladder graduated to 3,200 meters and a simple blade front. The safety is nothing more than a hammer half-cock, though the lever does have a hinged lower portion that locks it into position and prevents the action from being accidentally opened.

For our evaluation we managed to locate an original Russian Model 95 in pretty good condition. It has been our experience that when these guns do turn up, they are generally well-used, however our specimen exhibited a fair amount of original finish, good wood, a clean bore and crisp mechanism.

Ammo chosen was 147-grain LVE Russian sporting fodder. We were unable to locate a stripper clip, so could not determine how well the loading guide worked and were forced to press the rounds into the mag one at a time.

Initial offhand breaking-in shots proved the gun to be a good feeder and ejector, though recoil (even though the gun weighs some 9 pounds, 3 ounces) was pretty stout. The plain, curved steel buttplate did little to help.

We managed some pretty good sub-2-inch 100-yard rested groups using the original iron sights. The action was smooth, could be operated rapidly, and despite the stout recoil, target reacquisition was not bad. The trigger broke at just 7 pounds, after a light ⅜-inch takeup.

The fate of the Russian Winchesters following the Great War is as confusing as the Russian Revolution of 1917 was chaotic. Some rifles have been examined with the cartouche of Republican Spain, an indication that they were sold to aid in quelling the Civil War that erupted there in the late 1930s. Advertisements from early 1962 indicate that a quantity of Russian 95s were imported to the U.S. by Interarms and sold for $34.95. Today they command a premium if they can be found in any type of passable condition. Many have remarked that "if only it could talk, what stories it would tell."

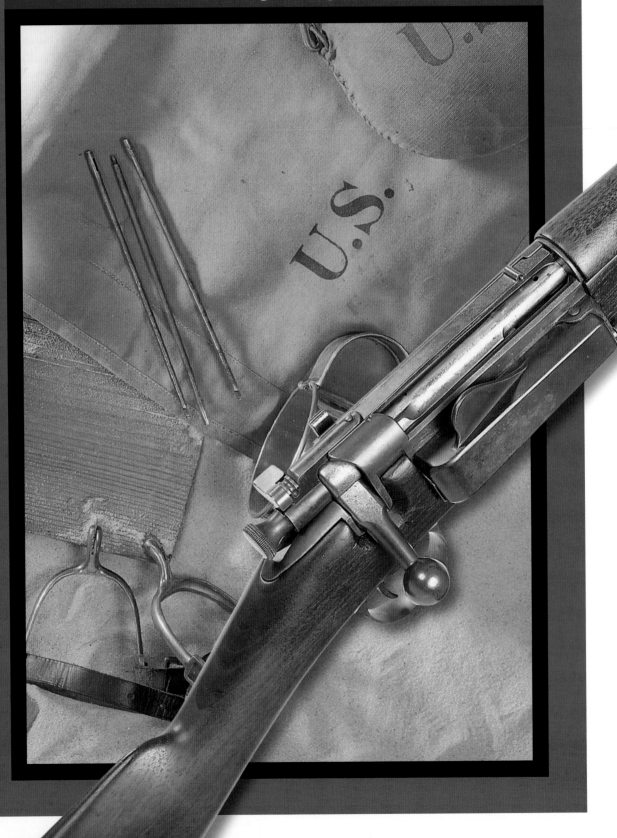

CLASSIC
TEST

This handy little repeater would
forever find fame as the arm carried by the
Rough Riders at the Battle of San Juan Hill.

Theodore Roosevelt called the Spanish-American War's Battle of San Juan Hill "my crowded hour." On July 1, 1898, the redoubtable Teddy, his Rough Riders and members of the 9th and 10th Regular Cavalry, among others, fought their way through a fusillade of Spanish Mauser bullets to capture a fortified blockhouse on top of Kettle Hill. The majority of his 1st U.S. Volunteers and the regular cavalry units carried carbine versions of the Army's first general-issue bolt-action repeating rifle, the .30-40 Krag-Jorgensen.

Despite the fact that many European powers had adopted small-bore magazine rifles as early as the mid 1880s, the United States felt content issuing single-shot black powder "Trapdoor" rifles to its troops well into the era of superior smokeless powder arms. Finally, the disparity in firepower and ballistics could not be ignored, and after extensive trials, in 1892 the War Department chose a modification of the Norwegian-designed Danish Krag-Jorgensen.

This bolt-action arm was fitted with an unusual side-mounted box magazine that (in the Danish Model) was opened by means of a long pivoting gate hinged at the front of the magazine. When the gate was opened, the follower was held back and five rounds could be placed into the aperture. Closing the gate released the follower and put pressure on the cartridges, forcing them one at a time into a position where they could be chambered by the gun's bolt.

The system was sure, reliable and extremely smooth. Only the single locking lug on the bolt head effected any limitation upon the gun, as it was too fragile to handle really hot loads.

The U.S. authorities generally were happy with the overall Krag-Jorgensen design; however, for American usage they felt compelled to incorporate a few changes. The magazine gate was modified to open downward, the bolt handle was turned down, a cutoff was incorporated so the gun could be fired single-shot and a better safety was added to the rear of the bolt. The caliber was reduced from .32 to .30.

The first M-1892 Krags were issued to troops

U. S. Model 1896 Krag-Jorgensen Carbine   **41**

30-40 KRAG CARBINE
150 SIERRA, 42.0 IMR 4895
WIN. LG RIFLE PRIMERS
100 YARDS

THE '96 PROVED TO BE A
SMOOTH, RELIABLE SHOOTER.
ROUNDS WERE CHAMBERED
AND EJECTED WITH EASE. THE
RIFLE'S RECOIL, INCIDENTALLY,
WAS VERY PLEASANT.

INSET: OUR EVALUATION KRAG CARBINE TURNED
IN EXCELLENT 100-YARD GROUPS, THOUGH
BECAUSE OF THE LIGHTER 150-GRAIN BULLET,
THEY CAME IN A LITTLE HIGH.

THE KRAG'S SAFETY IS SITED ON THE REAR OF
THE BOLT. ALL THE WAY TO THE RIGHT, THE GUN
IS READY TO FIRE, AND TO THE LEFT, "ON SAFE."

WHILE NOT AS FAST AS THE MAUSER STRIPPER-
CLIP SYSTEM, FIVE ROUNDS COULD BE DUMPED
INTO THE KRAG'S SIDE-MOUNTED BOX MAGAZINE
WITH RELATIVE EASE.

in 1894, and various other models of Krag rifles and carbines were introduced in 1896, 1898 and 1899. In 1898 a .22 Rimfire Gallery Practice Rifle allowed troops to practice marksmanship without expending expensive service ammunition.

The cartridge developed for use with the Krag was popularly known at the time as ".30 U.S." or ".30 Government," but its more common designation ".30-40" (denoting .30 caliber backed with 40 grains of smokeless powder) is the one familiar to modern shooters and collectors. Initial velocity of the 220-grain service load was 2,000 feet per second (fps)—a considerable gain in speed over the black-powder .45-70. In 1898 the velocity was increased to 2,200 fps, but given the hot, fast-burning powders and soft steels of the era, the boost did not work out—barrels were rapidly eroded and actions battered and damaged. Because of this, by 1903 the velocity was reduced to its original level.

The Krag was issued in time to see service in the Spanish-American War and while it performed well, it was realized that the slow side-loading magazine system was no match for the stripper-clip arrangement of the Spaniards' Model 1893 Mausers. This was most dramatically shown at the Battle of San Juan Hill, where some 700 Spanish riflemen inflicted 1,400 casualties on the attacking Americans (though it must be remembered that the *Yanquis* were attacking uphill against a fortified position).

Two years after the Spanish-American War, the Krag further distinguished itself in the hands of U.S. troops during the Boxer Rebellion in China, where it drew favorable comparison with the Enfields, Nagants, Lebels, Carcanos and Steyrs used by the other allied troops.

The Krag was also the principal military rifle of the long and bloody Philippine campaign. "And beneath the starry flag/ We'll civilize 'em with a Krag," went a line in a popular soldier's song of the period.

The subject of this piece, the Model 1896 Carbine, was a handy little repeater, well-suited for use on horseback. With a barrel length of 22 inches, and an abbreviated fore-end, the '96 was the first of the Krag carbines (a Model 1892 never went further than a prototype). It had a ring bar on the left side of the stock for the attachment of a carbine sling, as well as a trap in its butt to accommodate a screw-together cleaning rod. The rear, ladder-style sight was graduated to 2,000 yards, and the non-adjustable front blade was left unprotected, in the style of the period. Almost 20,000 Model '96 carbines were manufactured, but as many were altered to accommodate later changes, today it's hard to find an unaltered specimen.

Our evaluation '96 was in about 85 percent condition with a bright bore and much original bluing. A thin inspector's stock cartouche can still be seen on the wrist, and the gun even had its original three-piece cleaning rod and oiler in the butt trap. Ammunition used for the shoot was some handloads put up by my colleague Jeff John, which employed a 150-grain Sierra SP bullet backed by 42 grains of IMR 4895 giving us a muzzle velocity of some 2,400 fps.

Five rounds were duly dumped into the open magazine, the mag door shut and a round chambered. The Krag carbine certainly lived up to its reputation as having the smoothest bolt-actions ever. Throughout the session feeding and ejection was superb, and rounds could be fired in relatively rapid succession. Accuracy was excellent, though with the lighter bullets, groups were high. Average 100-yard, bench-rested spreads ran about 2¼ inches.

Even after the introduction of the 1903 Springfield, the Krag continued to be used by militia units and thousands were issued as training rifles during World War I. Following the conflict most were sold surplus and provided many a hunter with a low-cost, effective deer gun.

Stripping a Bolt

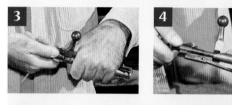

To strip a Krag bolt, first open the bolt and ensure the gun is unloaded. (1) Now lift up the extractor while lifting up on the bolt until it clears the receiver and align lug with receiver slot. (2) Remove bolt. (3,4) Pull head of firing pin shaft to rear and turn bolt body to separate. (5) Unlatch pin from shaft and slide off spring. (6) Unlatch and twist apart cocking piece and firing pin shaft from extractor.

*Japan's legendary
battle rifle was crude, quirky
and effective.*

The Japanese Arisaka was the brainchild of Col. Nariakira Arisaka. Essentially, there is but one basic Arisaka action, although there are two major models of rifle. The Type 38, introduced in 1905, was chambered for the semirimmed 6.5x50mm. The Type 99, introduced in 1939, was chambered in 7.7x58mm—also a semirimmed load.

The Type 38's 6.5x50 cartridge sent a .263-inch, 139-grain bullet out of the muzzle at 2,500 fps. Barrels featured a right-hand twist of one turn in 7.9 inches. The Type 99's 7.7x58mm cartridge featured a .313-inch, 175-grain bullet that left the muzzle at 2,400 fps. Barrels featured a right-hand twist of one turn in 7.88 inches. The Type 99 came in several versions, the most common being the long and short rifles. The long rifle featured a 31⅖-inch barrel, and the short rifle sported a 25½-inch barrel. There were also carbine variants with 19-inch barrels.

There was even a Type I rifle produced for the Japanese Navy in Italy combining features of the Model 1891 Mannlicher/Carcano rifle with the Type 38 Arisaka and chambered for the 6.5mm Japanese cartridge. I have one of these, and it is an improvement over the 1891 Mannlicher/Carcano in that it incorporates the Type 38 magazine rather than the Mannlicher clip-fed arrangement. My particular Arisaka/Carcano shoots pretty well.

Some Arisakas are among the strongest bolt-action rifles ever made. Others are probably less so. P.O.

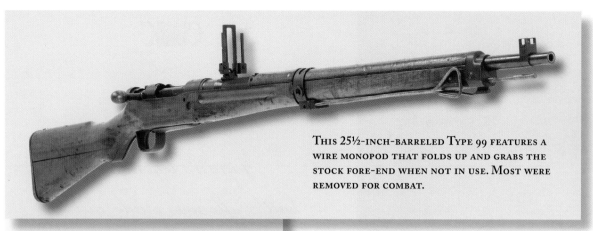

THIS 25½-INCH-BARRELED TYPE 99 FEATURES A WIRE MONOPOD THAT FOLDS UP AND GRABS THE STOCK FORE-END WHEN NOT IN USE. MOST WERE REMOVED FOR COMBAT.

THE REAR SIGHT OF THE ARISAKA FEATURES AN APERTURE REAR AS WELL AS A POP-UP LADDER FOR LONG RANGE (LEFT). IT ALSO FEATURES FOLDING ARMS TO COMPUTE LEAD WHEN IN USE AS AN ANTIAIRCRAFT SIGHT (RIGHT).

THE FRONT SIGHT IS AN INVERTED "V" POST THAT IS DRIFT-ADJUSTABLE FOR WINDAGE.

ARISAKA RIFLES EMPLOY DISTINCTIVE, LONG TOP AND BOTTOM TANGS IN THE GRIP AREA RATHER THAN THE TYPICAL RECOIL LUG FOUND ON MOST MAUSER DESIGNS. ALSO NOTE: THE CHECKERED BOLT-STRIKER SAFETY KNOB OF THE TYPE 99 HAS A CONCAVE CUT ON THE OUTSIDE RADIUS FOR EASY GRASPING.

Ackley in his *Handbook for Shooters and Reloaders* notes that the Type 38 action was in some ways better than the Mauser, Springfield and other designs of the time, and that the heat-treating was superior to that of other military actions.

No Arisaka will ever be accused of having a high degree of fit and finish. It is generally safe to say that when the trigger is pulled on an Arisaka with a round in the chamber, it will probably go bang. But this article is not intended to bash the Arisaka—I find them fascinating. But I also find them quite crude.

The Arisaka action features a five-round, staggered-box magazine; dual-opposed front locking lugs; and controlled-round feed via a massive nonrotating extractor. Like the 98 Mauser, the Arisaka has a third locking lug, and it also has another safety feature in that the bolt handle itself could serve as a last-ditch catch should all else fail. The knob at the rear of the bolt is pushed forward and clockwise to put the rifle on "safe." This also locks the bolt shut. To take the rifle off safe, push the knob forward, and rotate it a quarter-turn counterclockwise.

The safety knob is one of the more noticeable differences between a Type 38 and Type 99. On the Type 38 it is a convex bump on the outer circumference to aid in turning; on the Type 99 it is a concave cut. Another difference is in the floorplate system. On the Type 38, the release is in the front of the inside of the trigger bow, and the floorplate comes completely out when released. On the Type 99, the release is forward of the trigger, atop the inside of the trigger bow, and the floorplate itself is hinged.

Arisakas lack a recoil lug under the action.

Rather, there are long tangs top and bottom, extending from the rear of the action and along the top—and bottom—of the grip for several inches.

There are scads of sub-models known and identified. But with more than 6 million manufactured under such varied circumstances, all kinds of variations appeared.

Earlier production rifles featured a ladder-style rear sight that could be set for distances up to 1,500 meters. When it was in the down position, troops employed a nonadjustable aperture. On all but the last-ditch 99s, the rear sight included small arms that flipped out on each side of the ladder. These had notches to allow for lead when shooting at aircraft! The rear sight for last-ditch rifles was a simple, nonadjustable aperture. The front sight was an inverted "V" post that was drift-adjustable for windage and featured protective ears. Rifles made before 1942 came from the arsenal with a sliding dustcover over the ejection port as well as a folding, bent-wire monopod. Most dustcovers and monopods were discarded in combat.

Front receiver-ring markings identify the rifle as a Type 38 or Type 99. Originally, all had the Imperial chrysanthemum marking but most surrendered rifles had the 'mum ground off. Major arsenals that produced the Arisaka included Tokyo, Nagoya and Kokura, although there was production at other facilities. That is why, to my knowledge, there are no accurate production numbers. Suffice it to say that in order to outfit the Japanese army from the 1930s until 1945, the number was significant. Rifles made before 1942 had chrome-lined bores while ones made after that might not.

Arisaka stocks are generally made of very straight-grained wood. Two relatively thin pieces were dovetailed together lengthwise instead of using a single slab.

Surviving Arisakas with chrome-lined bores are usually in pretty good shape, despite cor-

BATTLE-RIFLE ROUNDS: THE 7.7MM ARISAKA CARTRIDGE (CENTER) IS FLANKED BY THE .30-06 (LEFT) AND THE .308 (RIGHT).

rosive-ammo. Chambers and bores, however, can range from pretty good to atrocious. Nominal specifications sometimes are little more than loose benchmarks. I have had a number of rifles with irregular chambers, some of them leaving the empty case bulged on one side due to poor quality control. Actual bore and groove dimensions also vary quite a lot from one production run to another.

Accuracy is, at best, ok. It is generally not difficult to shoot a two-inch group at 100 yards with an Arisaka, although it is rare to shoot one much under 1½ inches.

The feature rifle for this article was brought home as a war souvenir by a returning GI and it was doubtful the rifle saw much action, but it was used during Japan's "Great Pacific War."

WHEN TYPE 99 ARISAKAS WERE SURRENDERED AT THE END OF WORLD WAR II, THE IMPERIAL CHRYSANTHEMUM WAS OFTEN GROUND OFF.

ARISAKA STOCKS FEATURED STRAIGHT-GRAINED WOOD AND WERE CONSTRUCTED BY DOVETAILING TWO PIECES TOGETHER LENGTHWISE RATHER THAN USING A SINGLE SLAB OF WOOD.

CLASSIC TEST

This semi-auto eight-shooter was the best infantry rifle of World War Two.

Given the context of the statement, it's pretty hard to disagree with General George Patton's evaluation of the M 1 Garand, as "the greatest battle implement ever devised." While it achieved its greatest glory in World War II and Korea, the Garand in standard, sniper and match guises continues to be a favored arm with shooters worldwide.

When the rest of the world's armies were fielding bolt actions that were little changed from their counterparts in the Great War, the United States gave its infantrymen a rugged, reliable, accurate semi-auto. The "U.S. Rifle Caliber .30 M 1," as the Garand was officially called, was adopted into the service in 1936 after a rather tortuous birthing process. Its designer, John C. Garand, labored at the task for the Army Ordnance Department for almost 20 years before developing a design that was strong

THE M1 GARAND WAS UNQUESTIONABLY THE BEST INFANTRY RIFLE OF WORLD WAR II. IT WAS RELIABLE, HAD ADEQUATE FIREPOWER AND WAS QUITE ACCURATE.

enough to handle the formidable .30-06 round.

Though the gun went through several incarnations following its debut in the early 1930s, what finally appeared was a rifle that was deemed appropriate for the rough usage it could expect in the hands of a combat infantryman.

While today the system seems pretty obvious, when it first appeared Garand's design was hailed as something of a marvel. Using an eight-round, stamped sheet-steel en bloc clip as part of the feeding system, the rifle functioned as follows: The bolt handle was pulled to the rear, where the action was held open by the follower. A clip of ammo was pressed down into the magazine and the bolt allowed to move forward, where it stripped off and chambered a round. When the trigger was pulled and the round discharged, gases were tapped off through a gas port in the forward bottom part of the bore. These gasses forced the operating rod backward, compressing the operating rod spring and opening the bolt. As the bolt opened, it extracted and ejected the spent cartridge and cocked the hammer. Relaxation of the operating-rod spring now forced the bolt to move forward, where it stripped off and chambered the next round. When all eight shots had been expended, the clip was forcibly ejected from the action and the bolt remained open ready to receive another loaded clip.

Part of the magic of the rifle resided in its sturdy, responsive rotating bolt. Garand's system, proved to be so effective that it was used again in the selective-fire, removable-box-magazine 7.62mm M14 rifle—the gun that officially replaced the M1 in 1957.

The M1 was not only reliable, it was extremely accurate and was easily adapted to the sniping role. In addition, the M1 rapidly gained favor with competition shooters, and starting in the early 1950s, special National Match models were made up by Springfield Armory. Depending upon when they were put together, these guns will have glass-bedded stocks and specially fitted National Match parts.

Some six million Garands were produced by several sources between 1935 and 1957, including Springfield, International Harvester, Harrington and Richardson, and Winchester. Those guns produced by Springfield will have major components stamped "SA." International Harvester used the initials "IHC" (though barrels can be marked "LMR"). Winchesters are marked "WRA," and H&R used an "HRA" coding.

The M1's safety is a pierced piece of sheet metal located at the front of the triggerguard. Pushed to the rear, the gun is on "safe"—when

LOADING THE GARAND IS AS SIMPLE AS PRESSING AN EIGHT-ROUND CLIP OF AMMO INTO THE MAGAZINE. CALIBER OF THE GUN IS .30-06.

THE GARAND'S SAFETY IS A POSITIVE LEVER SET INSIDE THE FORWARD PORTION OF THE TRIGGERGUARD. TO PUT THE GUN ON "SAFE" THE LEVER IS PUSHED TO THE REAR. A SIMPLE PUSH WITH THE BACK OF THE TRIGGER FINGER READIES THE GUN FOR ACTION.

the lever is flicked forward, the gun is ready to fire. The M1's rear sight setup is pretty sophisticated, with a double-knurled-knob that corrects the peep for windage and elevation. The front sight is a blade, flanked by a pair of "wings." The butt has a compartment for an oiler and combination tool accessible via a trapdoor in the buttplate.

While not exactly a lightweight at 9½ pounds, the M1 Garand balances well and can be carried for extended periods with relative comfort. It shoulders nicely, and recoil, even with 150-grain ball ammo, is not prohibitive.

For our evaluation gun, we acquired a stock Garand, manufactured by Springfield in 1944. This rifle was tested with PMC 150-grain ball ammo, and 150-grain Samson SP. Targets were set up at 50 and 100 yards, though the wind was blowing at around 15 to 20 miles an hour, so I didn't hope for great accuracy at long range.

Functioning of the gun was excellent. It was shot offhand, rapid-fire and from a rest. Despite much tearing and blowing of targets, our 100 yarders weren't all that bad, with spreads coming in at an average of around 3 inches, with the best spread measuring 2⅝ inches. The top three-shot group of the day ran ½-inch at 50 yards from a bench. Functioning was perfect, and all who fired the piece proclaimed it a lot of fun. There are still lots of Garands out there and shooters are still reasonable, though some of the more exotic versions can cost upwards of several thousand dollars.

Fieldstripping

STRIPPING THE GARAND IS FAIRLY EASY. FIRST OPEN THE BOLT AND ENSURE THE GUN IS UNLOADED. (1) NEXT, PULL FORWARD ON THE TRIGGER GUARD AND REMOVE THE TRIGGER-GROUP. (2) NEXT, REMOVE THE BARREL/ACTION FROM THE STOCK. (3) PULL FORWARD ON THE FOLLOWER ROD, UNLATCH IT FROM THE FOLLOWER AND REMOVE IT AND THE SPRING FROM THE OPERATING ROD. (4) PUSH OUT THE FOLLOWER ARM SPRING (5) AND REMOVE THE BULLET GUIDE, FOLLOWER ARM, ROD CATCH AND FOLLOWER. (6) UNSCREW THE GAS CYLINDER PLUG USING AN M1 TOOL WRENCH OR SUITABLE SCREW-DRIVER (6,7) AND UNSCREW THE GAS CYLINDER LOCK AND SLIDE, PREPARATORY TO REMOVING THE GAS CYLINDER FROM THE BARREL. (8) FREE THE OPERATING ROD FROM ITS CHANNEL IN THE STOCK AND RECEIVER, CLEAR IT FROM THE BOLT AND REMOVE THE BOLT. (9) THE GUN IS NOW STRIPPED TO ITS BASIC COMPONENTS.

*Although it never replaced the
mighty M1, this intriguing artifact set the stage
for the concept of a "special operations" weapon.*

I first heard about the Johnson semi-automatic rifle at a tender age. My father had been a WWII Marine Paratrooper. Dad told me about places like Camp Eliott, New Caledonia and Vella La Vella in the Solomon Islands.

The Marine Parachute Regiments were eventually disbanded along with the Raiders, and Dad was reassigned to the 28th Regiment, Fifth Marine Division at Camp Pendleton (along with many other Paramarines and Raiders). From there he was shipped off to Iwo Jima to take part in what he always referred to as "The Great Conflict."

Anyway, Dad spoke often of two weapons he'd trained with in the Paratroops. First was the .45-caliber Reising submachine gun, of which he (and others) had a rather low regard. The second was the .30-caliber Johnson semiauto-matic rifle, a weapon that was manufactured in Providence, Rhode Island, and saw use with the Paratroopers and Raiders in the South Pacific.

Aesthetically, the Johnson made the M1 look positively sleek. Its pregnant-looking receiver with a stamped metal bellyband made the midsection look somewhat like a cigar. The unshrouded barrel looked naked and, well, whippy. On top of that, it had a ventilated metal handguard, sort of like an overgrown Ruger Ranch Rifle. Pretty Buck Rogers for its time indeed.

Instead of the eight-shot en bloc clip of the M1, the Johnson employed an integral 10-round rotary magazine that could be charged quickly with two Springfield '03 five-round stripper clips through the loading port on the right side of the receiver. The Johnson could also be quickly loaded with single cartridges, allowing the user to "top off" the magazine at will. From the prone position, the Johnson could be loaded without the shooter having to shift the rifle or, more important, raise his head.

In a 1996 copy of my father's February issue of *The Opening Shock*, a journal for the Association of Survivors of World War II Marine Parachute Regiments, former Marine

E<small>ARLY IN</small> W<small>ORLD</small> W<small>AR</small> II, <small>THE</small> U.S. M<small>ARINE</small> C<small>ORPS</small> <small>TOOK OVER STOCKS OF THE</small> J<small>OHNSON RIFLE ORIGINALLY</small> <small>MANUFACTURED FOR THE</small> D<small>UTCH.</small> D<small>ESIGNATED THE</small> M 1941, <small>THE RIFLE WAS USED TO ARM</small> M<small>ARINE PARA-</small> <small>CHUTISTS BECAUSE IT COULD BE BROKEN DOWN FOR</small> <small>COMPACT CARRY DURING A PARACHUTE DROP.</small>

THE JOHNSON (TOP) FAILED TO SUPPLANT THE LEGENDARY M1 GARAND (BELOW) IN THE HEARTS AND MINDS OF U.S. ARMY BRASS.

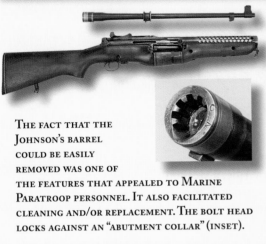

THE FACT THAT THE JOHNSON'S BARREL COULD BE EASILY REMOVED WAS ONE OF THE FEATURES THAT APPEALED TO MARINE PARATROOP PERSONNEL. IT ALSO FACILITATED CLEANING AND/OR REPLACEMENT. THE BOLT HEAD LOCKS AGAINST AN "ABUTMENT COLLAR" (INSET).

THE JOHNSON'S SAFETY IS JUST FORWARD OF THE TRIGGER-GUARD. THAT BULBOUS STEEL "BELLYBAND" ENCASES THE 10-SHOT ROTARY MAGAZINE.

Joe Aiello argued:

"In my opinion, and others', it was the best rifle of the three. I believe the only reason the Johnson was not adopted was that the Army already had thousands of Garands, and it wouldn't have been politically correct to throw them out."

This wouldn't have surprised Melvin M. Johnson, the rifle's designer. He was convinced his design was superior to that of the M1. Johnson felt that the M1's long operating rod could be easily bent, the gas trap mechanism was prone to fouling and the fact that most of the barrel was encased in wood would pro-mote overheating. He was convinced that a short-recoil system, such as that used in the Remington Model 8 was definitely superior.

Before the war, Johnson tried to get the Army to replace the Garand with his rifle, and field trials were held in December 1939. At their conclusion, the Army's evaluation listed several significant strengths—and weaknesses—of the rifle. On the plus side, it could be disassembled and assembled quickly without specialized tools; the barrel could be easily removed for cleaning or replacement; it proved functionally reliable in sandy conditions; and it was "reasonably" accurate. The negatives? The Johnson weighed more than 10 pounds (about a pound more than the M1); the recoil was perceived as no less than that of the bolt-action '03 Springfield; and the absence of a handguard made it "poorly suited" to bayonet fighting. The gas-operated M1 had prevailed, and the rest, as they say, is history.

But the Marine Corps was interested in the Johnson Rifle and the Johnson Light Machine Gun, a select-fire variant featuring a bipod and curved, side-mounted 20-round magazine. In 1943 the First Parachute Regiment procured 243 Johnson M 1941 rifles and 261 Johnson LMGs. But the Johnsons hadn't been made specifically for the USMC. They'd been purchased from the Netherlands Purchasing Commission, which had contracted Johnson Automatics Inc. to build them for the Dutch military.

In July 1942 the War Department finally contracted for 12,500 Johnson LMGs and

124,100 rifles, but in October of that year the order was terminated. The reason was that the government simply decided to bolster production of the bolt-action M 1903 A3 as a supplemental service rifle, and that increased production of the Browning Automatic Rifle virtually eliminated the need for a supply of Johnson LMGs.

It turns out, however, that old Paramarines and Raiders aren't the only fans of the Johnson. My friend Thomas Mackie, a connoisseur of U.S. military small arms of WWII vintage, is a major-league Johnson afficionado. Better still, he owns one that isn't minty enough to preclude a range session.

Thomas and I took the Johnson to the range and gave it a considerable workout with 1950s GI ammo, some 165-grain Speer Nitrex loads and some PMC Gold Line loads featuring 165-grain X-HP bullets. We set up our target at 100 yards and began to shoot at a gong with FN surplus ammo just to get the feel of things—which we did after 100 rounds or so. I was mightily impressed with the Johnson's reliability, nothing even resembled a malfunction, although that mushy, 6-pound trigger (a single-stage unit) required getting used to.

One thing I quickly learned was to resist the temptation to "ride" the bolt while charging the rifle. Although earlier Johnsons had a bolt "hold open" feature, this one didn't. I quickly learned to simply load the magazine, pull the bolt back and let 'er fly. The sights, incidentally, consist of an M1-style front blade protected by large ears and a fully adjustable aperture rear graduated to 1,000 meters. They're excellent, rugged and easy to acquire.

Our results on paper were about on par with what you'd expect from a vintage M1. The two sporting loads didn't group worth a whoop, but that old FN ball ammo did pretty good; with it, our five-shot 100-yard efforts ran between 4½ and 5 inches. We did have a couple of two-shot groups of around an inch or so, but the rifle simply wouldn't lay that third one in, no matter how hard we tried.

Taking the barrel off the Johnson for cleaning is a snap. First, verify that it's unloaded. Place the butt of the rifle on the floor, and push down slightly on that recoiling 22-inch barrel. As you're holding it down, insert a small punch (use a .30 cartridge tip if you feel like being authentic) into the hole on the right side of the fore-end about four inches back of the sling swivel. As you push it in firmly, it should release the springloaded locking lever. The barrel can now be pulled out easily.

Whatever weaknesses the Johnson may have had in comparison to the Garand, one thing remains clear today: The Johnson is a fascinating piece of WWII ordnance and a lot of fun to shoot.

THE JOHNSON SEMIAUTOMATIC RIFLE COULD BE LOADED BY STRIPPER CLIP (LEFT) OR WITH SINGLE CARTRIDGES (RIGHT).

THE JOHNSON FEATURES A FULLY ADJUSTABLE APERTURE REAR SIGHT (LEFT) AND AN M1-STYLE POST FRONT (RIGHT) WITH STURDY, PROTECTIVE "EARS."

*The 1878 Sharps Borchardt
was among the first of famed Hugo Borchardt's designs.*

No other 19th century firearm looks as modern today as the 1878 Sharps Borchardt. Ninteenth century target shooters were impressed by the rifle's trim, sleek appearance, but many were nonplussed by its lack of an external hammer or double triggers. It was made for a scant few years—1877 to 1881—and was doomed not only by the day's thirst for repeating rifles, but by the Sharps Rifle Co.'s inability to acquire sound financing. It is still considered one of the five strongest single shot rifle actions ever designed.

Only a few more than 22,000 Sharps Borchardt rifles were made. Originally designed for military sales, more than 11,000 '78 Sharps rifles were produced as muskets for U.S. militia and Chinese Army contracts. The balance were made up as sporting, target and express models. As soon as sporting rifles were offered, complaints by hunters followed. Its lack of a hammer or a set trigger proved a detriment to the rifle's acceptance. Borchardt eventually designed a factory set trigger mechanism, but it was inferior to those provided on the Sharps, Marlin Ballard and Remington rifles.

Still, the 1878 Sharps was a sturdy, rugged firearm that was revered for its strengths long after the demise of the Sharps Rifle Co. Its coil-spring powered striker-fired mechanism offered extremely fast lock time—the firing pin fall was a mere ⅜-inch—a fact lost on neither the sophisticated target shooters of the day or the varmint rifle builders of the 1950s. As well, most target shooters were constrained by rules that only allowed the use of a single trigger and the '78's was factory adjusted to a 3- or 3½-pound pull.

After the company's demise, the Borchardt Sharps remained well liked as a platform for custom rifles during the late 19th and early 20th centuries. As big-bore long-range target shooting fell from favor, men such as Harry

THE 1878 SHARPS BORCHARDT RIFLE WAS NEVER POPULAR WITH THE AVERAGE RIFLEMAN. NONETHELESS, ITS INHERENT STRENGTH AND QUICK LOCK-TIME FOUND FAVOR NOT ONLY WITH THE DAY'S TARGET SHOOTERS, BUT WITH CUSTOM RIFLE MAKERS FOR THE NEXT 100 YEARS.

THE SHARPS BORCHARDT SPORTING RIFLE (TOP) NEVER ACHIEVED THE POPULAR RECOGNITION UNTIL WELL AFTER THE DEMISE OF THE COMPANY.

CUSTOM 'SMITHS SUCH AS A.O. ZISCHANG OF SYRACUSE, NEW YORK, BUILT BEAUTIFUL TARGET RIFLES BASED ON THE BORCHARDT LIKE THIS .32-40.

THE MINUTE NOTCH OF THE STANDARD 1878 SHARPS REAR SIGHT WAS TOUGH TO ACCESS AND THE SLIDER ON THE REAR SIGHT IS UNMARKED FOR RANGE.

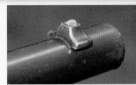

THE FRONT SIGHT WAS A PIECE OF GERMAN SILVER SET INTO A STEEL BASE. WELL MADE, IT TOO WAS A SMALL AFFAIR THAT MATCHED THE REAR SIGHT IN UTILITY.

THE BARREL MARKINGS OF THE 1878 SHARPS INCLUDE THE TRADITIONAL "OLD RELIABLE" TRADEMARK. LATER PRODUCTION '78S HAVE A BROKEN BORDER AROUND THE TRADEMARK. IN THE COMPANY'S FINAL DAYS, THE DIE WASN'T USED AT ALL.

OUR '78's 2¾-LBS. TRIGGER ALLOWED ACCURATE OFF-HAND SHOOTING. THE 10-LB. RIFLE IS WELL-BALANCED AND QUICK TO SHOULDER. THE BROAD STEEL SHOTGUN BUTTPLATE DISTRIBUTES RECOIL EVENLY.

Pope, George Schoyen and A. O. Zischang turned out remodeled mid-bore rifles in various .32 and .38 calibers for 200-yard shooting. Later, in the 1950s, a whole cottage industry sprang up and 'smiths began customizing the '78 for high-pressure varmint cartridges.

The Borchardt's is arguably the best single shot design of its era. Its stock was held to the receiver by a sturdy through-bolt, which is not only the strongest method, but necessary for a single shot rifle to stay consistently accurate. The receiver thoroughly supported its breech-block and the parts were big and simple. The Borchardt's smallest chambering was the .40-50-260 Sharps cartridge and the largest was the .45-100-550 Sharps.

The rifle itself is simple to use. Pulling down the Borchardt's triggerguard-lever cocks the striker, sets the safety (the little trigger at the back of the trigger guard) and extracts the empty shell far enough for it to fall out of the chamber. A new cartridge is easily loaded in the large trough in front of the chamber.

Our test 1878 rifle is a standard sporting rifle chambered for the .45-70 Government cartridge. Only about 1,600 sporting models are listed in the Sharps Co. records, although many serial number entries were never filled out and ours is one such rifle. The '78 is mechanically

INSET: PULLING DOWN THE TRIGGER-GUARD-LEVER OF THE BORCHARDT COCKS THE STRIKER, EXTRACTS THE SHELL AND RESETS THE SAFETY. IT IS QUICK AND POSITIVE AND THE BIG LOADING TROUGH ALLOWS FOR EASY RECHARGING.

tight and its barrel has a great bore with just a little pitting ahead of the chamber. The bore measures .460-inch at the breech and tapers quickly to .458-inch.

The 10-pound .45-70 Borchardt has a crisp 2¾-pound trigger and broad shotgun butt. Two black powder loads were assembled. The first and most accurate one consisted of a 500-grain .458-inch RN bullet cast with an RCBS BPCS mold from 20-1 lead. It was loaded over 52-grains of GOEX Ctg black powder in a Winchester case, one Walters vegetable fiber wad between bullet and powder, all set off by a Federal 215 magnum primer. The second load was similar to the U.S. Army's carbine load. This was a 405-grain .458-inch bullet over 55-grains of GOEX Ctg and a Federal 215 Magnum primer. The third load was the Black Hills Cowboy Action smokeless offering consisting of a 405-grain RNL bullet.

All the loads shot well, with the 500-grain load delivering an impressive 3-shot group of just 1⅛ inches. The biggest was the smokeless Black Hills load at 3¾ inches. We felt that was probably because the hard lead .458-inch bullet rattled down the first few inches of bore, while the bullets over black powder were bumped up to fill the grooves. A blow tube was employed between shots. As expected, there were no malfunctions and the action loaded and extracted flawlessly.

No hot loaded .45-70 ammo nor any jacketed bullet loads were used. Although the breeching strength of the Borchardt is legendary, its large firing pin and firing pin hole can cause trouble with high pressure loads. Also, the soft steel barrels of its day were never designed for such chamber pressures, and one risks chamber bulging or a stuck firing pin if things get out of hand.

The Sharps Borchardt rifle was the last of the fabled gun company's products. With the buffalo gone and the rising demand for repeating rifles, the company could not survive. Hugo Borchardt eventually moved to Germany where his repeating pistol designs were taken more seriously. Georg Luger took notice of Borchardt's ideas and the rest is history.

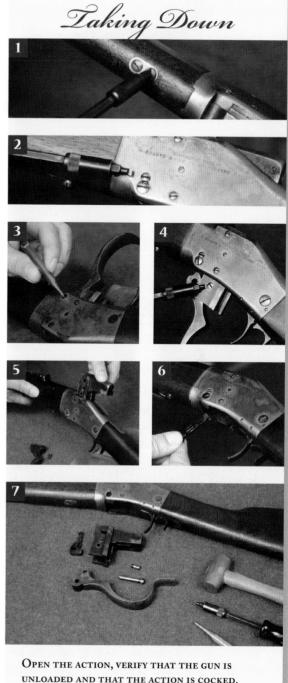

Taking Down

OPEN THE ACTION, VERIFY THAT THE GUN IS UNLOADED AND THAT THE ACTION IS COCKED. (1) LOOSEN THE MAINSPRING SCREW UNDER THE FORE-END. (2) TURN THE LEVER PIN CAPTURE SCREW UNTIL ITS CUTOUT FREES THE LEVER PIN. (3) DRIFT THE LEVER PIN OUT FROM THE OPPOSITE SIDE. (4) PULL THE LEVER OUT FAR ENOUGH TO REMOVE THE LEVER-LINK SCREW AND REPLACE THE LEVER PIN TO HOLD THE EXTRACTOR. (5) WITHDRAW THE BREECHBLOCK OUT FROM THE TOP. (6) REMOVE THE LEVER PIN AND EXTRACTOR. (7) THE SHARPS BORCHARDT DISASSEMBLED.

*This Browning-designed
pump-action may well be the
slickest rimfire hunting rifle ever made.*

The late 19th century pump-action "gallery gun" embodies an era when rifle marksmanship was deemed a most desirable and socially acceptable skill. The classic specimen was undoubtedly Winchester's Browning-designed Model 1890. This remarkably slick little slide-action was the direct predecessor to the company's revered Model 61 Hammerless and visible-hammer Model 62. Between 1890 and 1932, more than 849,000 Model 1890s were manufactured. The first 15,000 were solid-framed; the remainder of the run being made in takedown configuration.

S.P. Fjestad's *Blue Book of Gun Values* makes note of the fact that because so many of them were so heavily used in shooting galleries, specimens in anything resembling mint condition are rare. During its heyday, according to Ned Schwing in *Winchester Slide-Action Rifles* (Vol. 1), "More people were exposed to the Model 90 than any other .22 caliber rifle in America."

Every once in awhile we get the opportunity to shoot a gun with some history, and our particular 1890 Winchester, owned by Otto Meyer, is just such a gun. Meyer was a trick shot and trick roper for Buffalo Bill's

Wild West show at the turn of the century. In 1910, he went to work for Gaston Melies as an actor and stuntman for Melies Star Film Co. in San Antonio, Texas. Meyer followed Melies to California, where he married a judge's daughter and settled down. Gaston Melies left California with some of his film company in 1912, never to return. Otto Meyer stayed and purchased this 1890 for use on his Culver City, California ranch in the late 1920s. He was shepherding as well as horse wrangling and doing stunt work for the fledgling movie industry. Otto gave his son, Ben, the Winchester in the late 1930s. Ben Meyer used it to protect the flock from coyotes and other predators for the next 25 years or so when he was running sheep from Culver City over the mountains to Encino, west through the foothills of Calabasas and north to what is now the burgeoning city of Santa Clarita. Now, 60 years later, civilization has all but obliterated the old sheep trails and replaced them with clogged freeways and suburban homes. When far from home, Ben also used the M1890 to take deer for himself and the other herders as the occasion arose, although rarely

ALTHOUGH SOME M 1890S WERE SOLID-FRAMED, OUR SPECIMEN WAS A TAKEDOWN MODEL, WHICH SIMPLY REQUIRES LOOSENING THE FRAME-MOUNTED SCREW TO FACILITATE CLEANING, STORAGE OR TRANSPORT.

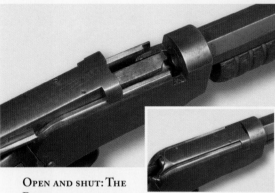

OPEN AND SHUT: THE BROWNING-DESIGNED PUMP-ACTION OF THE MODEL 1890 IS SLICK AND FAST-CYCLING. WE EXPERIENCED NO MALFUNCTIONS WITH OUR WELL-USED TEST RIFLE.

THE FOLDING MARBLE'S TANG PEEP IS TAILOR-MADE FOR THE TRIM LITTLE WINCHESTER MODEL 1890—ENHANCING THE RIFLE'S SHOOTING QUALITIES WITHOUT SACRIFICING ITS 19TH CENTURY CHARM.

with the consent of the prevailing officials. He preferred the .22 WRF because it had more power than other .22 rimfires, yet was quiet and plenty accurate enough (and still is) to make behind-the-ear shots on unwary mulies. The M1890 also filled the pot with plenty of rabbits and other small game.

Externally, our 1890 shows the wear of a gun that has spent many a day and night in the field as a herder's gun. Upon receiving it, it was also apparent that it hadn't been cleaned in decades, and the stock had been broken in several places. We put a Bore Snake down the horrible-looking bore and gave it yank. A shower of dried oil and gunk flew from the barrel and upon peering down the tube afterward, we were amazed and pleased to find it in pristine condition. A detail strip-and-clean followed and most of the dried oil and grit were bathed away, restoring the action to its legendary smoothness. The stock has been repaired with Crazy Glue until a more permanent repair is accomplished.

Prior to his death, Ben Meyer had told of his affection for this rifle, and despite the outward appearance, he had carefully cleaned it before putting it away when he fired his last round of .22 WRF ammo sometime in the late 1960s. Externally, the metal is well worn with most of the finish gone and the light surface pitting is from bad storage in the last 20 or 30 years.

Winchester made its 1890 rifles available in .22 Short, Long and .22 WRF. This was prior to the creation of the .22 Long Rifle, and the .22 WRF substantially increased the killing power of the available rimfire rounds. This relatively high-powered .22 drove a 40- or 45-grain .224-inch projectile at 1,450 fps. It used an inside lubricated bullet rather than the conventional rimfire's outside lubricated heel-based bullet. Such ammunition stayed cleaner when carried loose in the pockets.

The cartridge has long been obsolete, and modern .22 Long Rifle high-velocity ammunition comes very close to the WRF's top performance. Indeed, when we chronographed the M1890 with some recent Winchester Commemorative .22 WRF ammo, we found it rather anemic—the 45-grain bullet exiting our test rifle's 24-inch octagonal barrel at a leisurely 1,250 fps or so. Perhaps Winchester feels that there are enough marginal guns are out there to keep the speed and pressures down a bit. No guns have been made for this cartridge since before World War II, so Winchester may have a point. Still, the .22 WRF is a most enjoyable cartridge to shoot and plenty accurate enough for

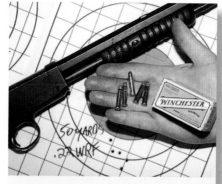

THIS FIVE-SHOT, 50-YARD, 1¼-INCH GROUP TESTIFIES TO THE ACCURACY OF THE MODEL 1890. THE AMMO USED WAS FROM A LIMITED RUN OF WINCHESTER COMMEMORATIVE .22 WRF FROM THE AUTHOR'S PERSONAL STASH.

small game to boot.

To take full advantage of the little rifle's potential during the range session, we installed one of Marble's excellent peep tang rear sights on it and then removed the open rear sight and installed a slot blank to fill the gap. Whatever doubts we had as to how this history-rich old timer would perform evaporated immediately. At 50 yards, 5-shot groups averaged 1½ inches, with several coming in at just a hair over an inch. That's excellent for a receiver-sighted .22 of any action or vintage, let alone an old pump chambered for what is essentially a hunting load (and the only load available to boot). Functioning was flawless throughout, thanks, no doubt, to our initial cleaning efforts.

Any shooter who automatically equates new with good should work this action—it has that slick, well-worn smoothness that only time, and thousands of rounds—can provide. The extremely short throw of the slide requires just a flick of the wrist. In all, five shooters handled and shot it during the course of our shoot, and at the end of the day, everyone wanted it. Used and well battered, with plenty of local color behind it, this particular Model 1890 bears out the traditionalist's lament, "They certainly don't make 'em like they used to."

THE .22 WRF (CENTER) RANKS IN POWER SLIGHTLY ABOVE THE .22 LONG RIFLE (LEFT) AND CONSIDERABLY BELOW THE .22 WMR (RIGHT). IT'S QUITE ACCURATE AND AN EXCELLENT SMALL-GAME LOAD.

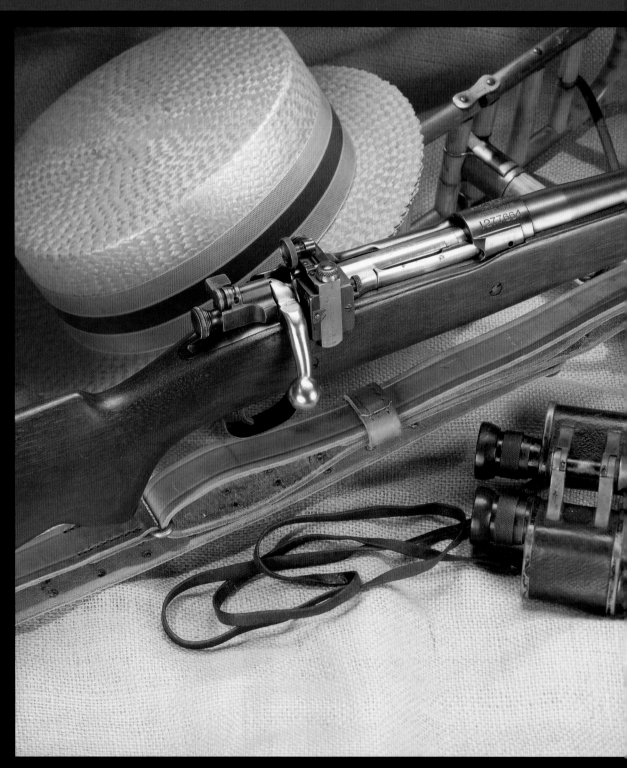

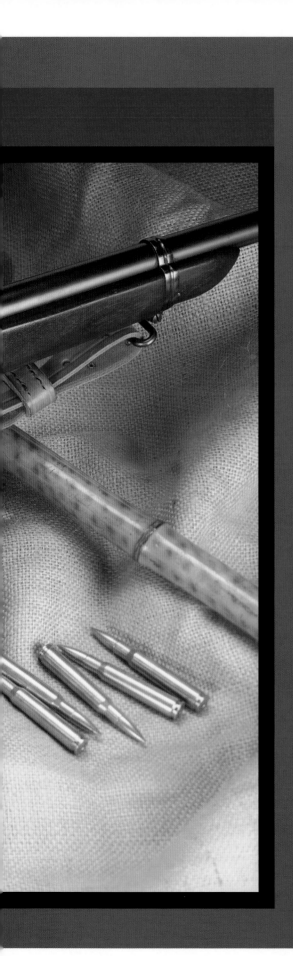

*This national
match-grade '03
raised the military .30
to new heights.*

Someone once said that the Model 98 Mauser was a hunting rifle, the Mark III SMLE a battle rifle, and the 1903 Springfield a target rifle. As the '03 was basically a Mauser-style action, this is a double tribute to the 98, but the Yankee Springfield added a few wrinkles of its own—good and bad.

The '03, as its name implies, was adopted in 1903 as a replacement for the well-made but flawed Krag-Jorgensen. Designers took the Mauser action and replaced the single firing pin with a two-piece unit. While a broken pin could be more easily fixed, the modification caused the assembly to be somewhat weaker than the original.

In addition, the gun's breeching setup owed more to the Krag than the Mauser, resulting in less case support and some gas control problems. It was also fitted with a magazine cutoff—an arrangement that was in vogue at the time, but proved to be pretty much a fifth wheel. The cutoff prevented rounds from being stripped off from the magazine and allowed it to be fired single shot.

The rifle that appeared in 1903 had a full-length walnut stock, blued barrel and other metal parts,

A MAGAZINE CUTOFF ON THE LEFT SIDE OF THE ACTION ALLOWS THE RIFLE TO BE FIRED SINGLE SHOT. AT MIDPOINT, THE LEVER ALLOWS THE BOLT TO BE REMOVED FROM THE GUN.

THE GUN'S SERIAL NUMBER IS ADDED TO THE BOLT WITH AN ELECTRIC PENCIL.

A HEAVILY CHECKERED SHOT-GUN-STYLE CURVED BUTTPLATE REPLACED THE THINNER, STRAIGHT MILITARY VERSION. THERE IS NO TRAP IN THE BUTT FOR CLEANING GEAR.

case-hardened receiver and a sophisticated ladder sight. An unusual feature was an integral rod-style bayonet that harkened back to a similar design on the Model 1884 "Trapdoor" rifle. President Theodore Roosevelt looked at the gun and, while he was pleased with it, made some suggestions that resulted in a somewhat changed—and improved—version that appeared some two years later. The new gun dispensed with the fragile rod bayonet and incorporated a lug for a more conventional blade. The rear sight was also changed and made more robust and user-friendly.

The round developed for the 1903 was a Mauser-style rimless cartridge that fired a 220-grain cupro-nickel-jacketed roundnose .30 bullet at some 2,300 feet per second (fps). Following the adoption by the Germans of a 154-grain spitzer bullet that had a muzzle velocity of 2,880 fps, U.S. Ordnance officials began rethinking our 1903 round and came up with an improved version with a 150-grain spitzer bullet and MV of 2,700. The new "Model 1906" (or .30-06) case was .070 inch longer than its predecessor and more than lived up to its promise as a military round. With various loadings it became one

KNURLED KNOBS ALLOW THE LYMAN 48 SIGHT TO BE ADJUSTED FOR ELEVATION AND WINDAGE. AFTER A BIT OF INITIAL FIDDLING, WE HAD THE GUN SHOOTING TO POINT OF AIM AT 100 YARDS.

FRONT SIGHT ON THE '03 SPORTER IS SIMILAR TO THE MILITARY SIGHT. THE RAMP HAS BEEN STRIATED TO REDUCE GLARE.

TO PUT THE GUN ON SAFE, THE LEVER IS PUSHED ALL THE WAY TO THE RIGHT. THIS IS SIMILAR TO THE MAUSER SYSTEM, WHICH THE SPRINGFIELD EMULATES.

of the world's preeminent hunting rounds and a not too bad targeteer.

There is little question that the improved 1903 Springfield was one of the handsomest military rifles ever designed. It worked well and saw early use in the Philippines, Mexico and in World War I.

The '03 proved to be versatile. Modifications such as an Air Service version with a 25-round extension magazine and chopped stock to be carried in observation balloons were essayed, as was a modification of the gun that could be fitted with a semi-automatic "Pedersen Device." A pretty good sniper version topped with a prismatic Model 1908 Warner-Swazey scope saw some use in France.

It was recognized early on that the '03 Springfield was no slouch on the target range, and moves were made to improve the rifle for competition. Several National Match models were developed, one of the more popular being the NRA Sporter introduced in 1924.

Manufactured at Springfield Armory, this rifle could be purchased by National Rifle Association members. The original cost of the gun was a not insubstantial $50.84, which was reduced to $42.50 by 1932. It sported a 1922-style half-stock with pistol grip and no finger grooves, a National Match-quality action, a heavy star-gauged barrel, and steel shotgun-style buttplate. The military sight was replaced with a Lyman 48 receiver peep. While the rifle was finished in the manner of the military arm, the bright bolt had a serial number electric-pencilled on the body. Some 6,500 of these guns were made between 1924 and 1933, when Springfield ceased manufac-

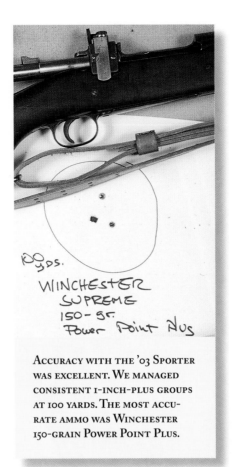

ACCURACY WITH THE '03 SPORTER WAS EXCELLENT. WE MANAGED CONSISTENT 1-INCH-PLUS GROUPS AT 100 YARDS. THE MOST ACCURATE AMMO WAS WINCHESTER 150-GRAIN POWER POINT PLUS.

ture. There was enough competition from private companies such as Griffin & Howe to make the venture redundant.

Like its martial brother, the NRA Sporter had a three-position safety mounted on the rear of the bolt, a cutoff and knurled cocking piece. To put the gun on safe, the tab is moved to the right. A central, vertical position keeps the gun on safe but allows the bolt to be withdrawn.

The NRA '03 Sporter that we selected for our evaluation was a pristine example that had obviously seen little use. The bore was perfect and the relatively unstagey trigger came in at an agreeable 2½ pounds.

Sighting on the gun, as per original specs, consisted of a Lyman Model 48 with knob adjustments for elevation and windage. The front sight was a military blade style.

Chosen ammunition for our evaluation was 143-grain PMP FJBT, 165-grain Federal Premium and 150-grain Winchester Supreme Power Point Plus. After a bit of fiddling with the sight, the gun hit pretty much to point of aim at 100 yards and gave consistent 1-inch-plus groups. Functioning was perfect. The gun was comfortable to shoot on the bench or off, and the heavily checkered, curved buttplate was a definite shooting aid.

Without question, the NRA Sporter was an absolutely lovely gun. Perhaps the thing that impressed me most about the piece was that it showed that it was actually possible for a private individual to purchase a high-quality sporting arm from a federal armory and that shooting sports were not only condoned but promoted by the government!

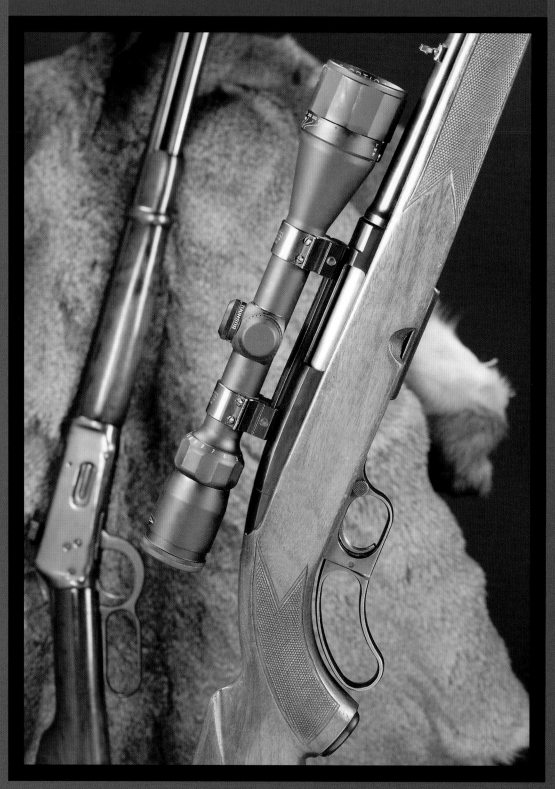

CLASSIC TEST

This sleek, thoroughly modern lever-action was ahead of its time.

Ever want a bolt-action rifle that handles like a slick lever gun? Just get a Winchester Model 88. The Model 88 features a three-lug, rotating bolt action that is cycled with an underlever that looks like that of a Model 99 Savage. And the Model 88 does all of this with the configuration and feel of a Model 70 Winchester, widely touted as "the rifleman's rifle."

During its production run from 1955 through 1973, there were roughly 284,000 (some list the number as 283,913) Model 88s made in .308, .243, .358 and .284. When introduced, the Model 88 was available only in .308. The next year—1956—two more chamberings were added: the .243 and the .358. And then in 1963 the .284 was introduced.

There was an interesting phenomenon afoot in the shooting industry in those early days of the Model 88 that, interestingly, parallels some of the things going on in the industry today. The Model 88 handled relatively short and fat cartridges compared to the "standard" car-

tridges of the day like the .30-06 and .270.

Some might opine that a rifle has achieved some degree of lasting relevance if it has had a cartridge specifically designed for it. Perhaps. But in the case of the Model 88, exactly half of the cartridges originally chambered to it are no longer in common use. And the .308 and .243 do not continue to enjoy popularity due to the Model 88; their popularity was unaffected when the rifle was dropped. In the end, the Model 88 never really set the sales world afire. (But it does pose a question: Why, when Winchester changed the Model 70 bolt-action rifle in 1964, didn't the company opt to have the new bolt-action feature three-lug lockup? After all, the Model 88 proved that the company knew how to make three lugs work. So why didn't Winchester add a shorter bolt lift to the features of the post-'64 Model 70?)

When the Model 88 was introduced, I was in awe. It seemed to embody everything I thought I ever wanted in a rifle. And it was chambered for that "new" .308 round. Wow! Deer in Michigan would never be safe again, I thought to myself.

Since then I've shot a number of Model 88s. Yet I own just one, a late-'50s .243. That's probably because of the difference between the dream and the reality of the Model 88. For me it's an "almost" rifle—a "coulda-been, shoulda-

SMOOTH-CYCLING TRANSITION: WINCHESTER PRODUCED MODEL 88s FROM 1955 TO 1973 IN VARIOUS "NON-TRADITIONAL" CALIBERS SUCH AS .243, .284, .308 AND .358 WINCHESTER. THE TRADITIONAL MODEL 94 (BACKGROUND) IS STILL VERY MUCH WITH US.

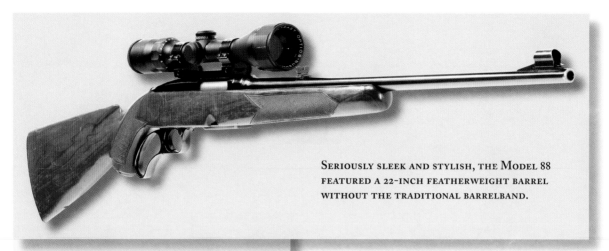

SERIOUSLY SLEEK AND STYLISH, THE MODEL 88 FEATURED A 22-INCH FEATHERWEIGHT BARREL WITHOUT THE TRADITIONAL BARRELBAND.

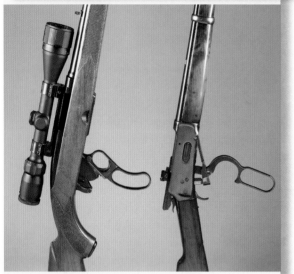

ACTION EVOLUTION: THE MODEL 88'S LEVER (LEFT) CYCLED A THREE-LUG ROTATING BOLT THAT PROVIDED MUCH GREATER POTENTIAL THAN THAT OF THE MODEL 94 (RIGHT).

been" kind of a thing. I must admit that I have shot some Model 88s that have been custom redone, and they are awesome. But the as-issued rifles always seemed to need some kind of qualifier injected into the conversation when they were discussed.

For example, the featherweight-barrel contour is a little whippy. Typically, it's not difficult to get a Model 88 to shoot somewhere in the 1.25- to 1.5-inch category at 100 yards. Mine will deliver 1.5- to 1.6-inch groups with most good ammo, but nothing much better—ever. But rarely is an as-issued Model 88 able to deliver an-inch-or-better groups. Some folks

blame the trigger, but it has always seemed that the barrel itself does well to do much better than 1¼ inches. Bear in mind, however, that the standard Model 70 of the same period typically delivered about the same-size groups, so there is no effort here to be unnecessarily harsh on the Model 88.

Speaking of the trigger, the kindest thing one can say about it is that when sufficient force is applied to it, it will allow the rifle to fire. That can, however, be remedied, so the issue need not be a deciding one for anyone who wants to shoot a Model 88 a lot.

The real joy of the Model 88 is that it handles quickly and points and swings superbly. In a hunting rifle, these are important things. And that's what the Model 88 is—a hunting rifle.

The lever mechanism/linkage on the Model 88 is unique. For one thing, the trigger and everything remains with the lever as it is cycled. When the action is cycled, the bolt is pulled rearward and then pushed forward, rotating the three-lug, front locking bolt at the end of the forward cycle. It works well and locks up great.

The magazine is a removable box design that holds four cartridges, which means that it's possible to carry five rounds (with one in the chamber). The beefy magazine release allows it to be removed with cold and/or wet hands.

Pre-'64 Model 88s feature diamond-cut checkering on the pistol grip and fore-end and a steel lever. For the most part, those made after 1964 featured non-ferrous levers and impressed basketweave checkering (as is often the case with old Winchesters, non-cataloged variations are encountered, so it's risky to make blanket statements about features). Barrels are 22 inches long, and there's no barrelband. In 1968 Winchester added the Model 88 carbine that featured no checkering, a barrelband and 19-inch barrel. The carbine was chambered in .308, .243 and .284.

Unlike traditional Winchester lever-actions, the Model 88 has a sleek, modern look with its contoured receiver and one-piece stock. It came drilled and tapped for scope mounting or for a rear aperture sight.

Perhaps one of its accuracy challenges is the way the barreled action is connected to the stock. There is one screw (bolt) holding the barrel to the fore-end about an inch forward of the rear sight. The rear of the barreled action is held in place by a steel fixture into which the rear of the action is keyed. Although this system is substantial, it can result in uneven torque on the barrel and action during firing if everything is not totally perfect.

The Model 88 was the product of a transitional era in the firearms industry. It could be argued that the late 1950s and early 1960s heralded the beginning of the modern era of sporting rifles. And the Model 88 was the industry's last, best shot at reviving the lever-action. In the same way that the Model 71 was the last of the Winchester lever rifles of the Browning design that fell to the Model 70 in the marketplace, the Model 88 lost the final round in the "high-intensity lever gun" contest.

By the time the Model 88 left the market, Savage's Model 99 lever-action was also in steep decline. Sako's Finnwolf spanned the same general period, having been introduced in 1962 and discontinued in 1974. Yet both Winchester and Marlin have continued to market traditional lever-actions in less intense chamberings. This has ensured that—within certain parameters—the lever-action lives on. But as a mainline rifle in competition with the bolt action, it's history. (In 1961 Winchester introduced the Model 100, a semiauto version of the Model 88. It, too, was dropped in 1973.)

Sadly, many Model 88s spend most of their

THE AUTHOR'S MODEL 88 IN .243 FEATURES DIAMOND CUT CHECKERING ON THE FORE-END AND A DETACHABLE FOUR-ROUND MAGAZINE (INSET).

ALTHOUGH DEFINITELY "SCOPE-FRIENDLY," THE MODEL 88 FEATURED A FOLDING LEAF REAR SIGHT.

THE AUTHOR STILL SHOOTS HIS MODEL 88. THIS THREE-SHOT, 100-YARD GROUP (INSET)—USING FEDERAL 100-GRAIN FACTORY LOADS—MEASURES 1⅝ INCHES, WHICH IS ABOUT PAR FOR THE RIFLE.

time these days in closets and gun vaults. They deserve better than that. They deserve to be hunted with, shot and enjoyed. The Model 88 is a true Winchester and one of the more interesting designs of its time. In its own way, it truly is a classic.

*Heir to the great Model 1886,
this modernized big-bore lever-action
is one of the classiest cult collectibles ever.*

According to an old cliché, "It's hard to improve on perfection." But that saying was proven wrong in 1935, when the first Winchester Model 71 was shipped from the factory. Up until then, the most popular big-game lever-action was the Winchester 1886, which possessed fortress-like strength due to an imposing receiver that housed twin vertical, sliding locking bolts.

This novel design was the first lever-action repeater developed for Winchester by firearms genius John Moses Browning. The rock-solid strength of the Model 1886 was such that it easily carried the rifle from black-powder cartridges into the smokeless-powder era.

But by the early 1930s it was obvious that

CHAMBERED IN .348 WINCHESTER, THE MIGHTY MODEL 71 WAS HEIR TO THE 1886. DESPITE THE FACT THAT IT'S BEEN OUT OF PRODUCTION (EXCEPT FOR A BRIEF RUN OF BROWNING COMMEMORATIVES) FOR 45 YEARS, ITS LUSTER REMAINS UNDIMMED.

in order to make the Winchester 1886 more appealing to a new generation of big-game hunters, it would have to be updated, not only mechanically, but in caliber. Hunters were demanding more powerful chamberings, but the Model 86 was only available in .45-70 and .33 Winchester, a pair of still-effective (but dated) cartridges.

Something newer was needed if Winchester was to maintain its lever-action reputation. Besides, the Model 86, with its massive metal-work and interlocking mechanics, had become an extremely expensive rifle to produce. As early as 1931 Winchester began working on a solution that would breathe new life into its legendary lever-action.

In anticipation, the Model 86 was discontinued in 1935. The rifle that emerged to replace it that same year was the Winchester 71, an "improved Model 86" chambered for the brand-new .348 Winchester, the most powerful rimmed cartridge available in a lever-action at that time.

A FAST, SMOOTH ACTION AND POSITIVE EJECTION MADE THE MODEL 71 THE ULTIMATE BIG-GAME RIFLE FOR LEVER-ACTION FANS.

ALTHOUGH .348 COMPONENTS ARE AVAILABLE FROM CUSTOM SHOPS AND BULLET SUPPLIERS, THE ONLY READILY FOUND FACTORY LOAD TODAY IS THE 200-GRAIN WINCHESTER SILVERTIP.

THE WINCHESTER MODEL 71 IS LOADED VIA THE LARGE GATE AT THE RIGHT SIDE OF THE RECEIVER. THE CAPACITY OF THE THREE-QUARTER-LENGTH TUBULAR MAGAZINE IS FOUR ROUNDS.

In overall appearance the Model 71 clearly retained its Model 1886 heritage and, in many ways, resembled a customized version of the old 86. But there were differences, both obvious and subtle. For one thing, the crescent steel buttplate of the 86 had been replaced by a less painful, flat, shotgun buttplate, or a factory-installed rubber recoil pad. Moreover,

the checkered, varnished stock and hand-filling semi-beavertail fore-arm promised better control. Whereas a capped pistol grip had been an extra-cost option on the 1886, it was now standard on the Model 71, along with a gracefully curved lever.

Beneath the 24-inch barrel was a three-quarter-length tubular magazine that held four cartridges; plenty for most hunting situations, especially with a fifth round in the chamber. Purchasers had a choice of either a semi-buckhorn Lyman 22K open rear sight or a bolt-mounted peep; later postwar Model 71s did away with the sometimes disconcerting bolt-mounted sight and instead incorporated a Lyman Number 56 peep fitted to the receiver. A hooded ramp front sight with steel post and bead remained standard throughout production.

The action had been simplified and strengthened. Complementing this rework, the flat springs of the Model 1886 were replaced by sturdier coil ones. That, plus stronger steel, made the 71 much more rugged than its stalwart precursor. Later versions featured a more perfected action with a split trigger-safety catch—similar to the Model 94—that prevented the hammer from being tripped until the lever was completely closed and locked. Of course, before that could happen, the bolt was already fully seated into the breech, making the Model 71 one of the safest rifles of its day.

This initial version is now called the "deluxe model" by collectors. From January 6, 1936 until 1947, a slightly lower cost, unchecked variant without a pistol-grip cap and sporting a 20-inch barrel was offered, which is now referred to as the Model 71 Carbine. Model 71s up to approximately serial number 15,000 had tangs that measured 3⅞ inches in length, and collectors have subsequently labeled these early rifles "long tang" models. Later guns had 2⅞-inch tangs and are called "short tangs," but these terms are strictly collector jargon, with no such official designations made by Winchester.

The .348 Winchester was the only chambering ever offered in the Model 71. Its case was based upon the .50-110 black-powder cartridge originally chambered in the Model 1886. In effect it was an improved .33 Winchester.

The .348 was initially offered by Winchester and Remington with 150-, 200- and 250-grain bullets. In retrospect, the 150-grain projectile was ballistically inferior, but the 200 and 250 grainers found immediate favor among deer, moose, elk and bear hunters.

No matter what weight bullet it was stoked with, the Model 71 was enthusiastically embraced by lever-action devotees. With its blunt-nosed bullets (required in a tubular magazine), the effective range of the new rifle-cartridge combination was limited to 200 yards, but that was more than adequate for its iron sights. It was considered heresy to outfit a Model 71 with a scope. After all, this rifle was specifically designed for close-range pursuit of the most dangerous North American game, where a fast follow-up shot might be needed.

Even though I was just a lad in high school and had never shot anything larger than a jackrabbit, the romantic lure of the Model 71 captivated me when I first read about it in 1958. That, unfortunately, was also the year it was discontinued, with 47,254 rifles having been produced.

As with the Model 1886 almost a quarter-century before, the high cost of manufacture and changing times finally brought the curtain down on this classic. But when a gunwriter, writing in some long-forgotten magazine, lamented the demise of the Model 71, referring to the rifle as "businesslike," I vowed to get a one for myself.

That day arrived many years later when I purchased a late production short-tang version with a receiver-mounted peep sight.

The current factory .348 200-grain load produces a muzzle velocity of 2,520 fps and a muzzle energy of 2,820 ft-lbs which, at 100 yards, drops to 2,178 ft-lbs. Certainly respectable, but in reality, it's on a par with the killing energy of a 180-grain .30-06 load. But with its slightly heavier 200-grain bullet, the .348 Winchester is certainly capable of taking any big-game animal with a well-placed shot.

As hunters and collectors continue to redis-

THE AUTHOR HAD NO TROUBLE MAINTAINING FIVE-SHOT, 2½-INCH GROUPS AT 100 YARDS WITH THIS APERTURE-SIGHTED MODEL 71. THE AMMUNITION USED WERE 200-GRAIN WINCHESTER SILVERTIPS.

EARLY MODEL 71S HAD A BOLT-MOUNTED PEEP THAT WAS REPLACED WITH A LYMAN NUMBER 56 MOUNTED ON THE RECEIVER (LEFT). FOR HUNTING, THE AUTHOR PREFERS TO REMOVE THE APERTURE FROM THE LYMAN 56 PEEP AND SIMPLY SIGHT THROUGH THE LARGER OPENING (RIGHT).

cover the old 71, demand has grown. As a result, Browning made a limited-edition run of Model 71 rifles and carbines in 1986.

Current factory loads include a 200-grain Winchester Silvertip and a 200-grain soft-point from Old Western Scrounger. In addition, Buffalo Bore has recently introduced a 250-grain jacketed flatnose. For handloaders, Hornady carries a 200-grain bullet and Barnes offers heavier 220- and 250-grain projectiles. Zeroed for 150 yards, the Winchester Silvertip shoots an inch and a half high at 100 yards and drops 3 inches at 200 yards.

At 100 yards I have no trouble shooting 3-shot, 1½-inch groups with this ammunition. I've yet to try my Model 71 on bear or elk, but when that time comes, I have no doubt that it will do the job. After all, you can't improve upon perfection.

Webley-Fosbery Revolver

This "automatic revolver" was a dead-end auto design that still managed to find some favor with target shooters and soldiers.

More than once, especially in old movies, one hears characters using the term "automatic revolver." Of course in 99 percent of the cases this is just poor writing. But at least once, in John Huston's 1940 film of Dashiell Hammett's *The Maltese Falcon*, the term was used correctly when Sam Spade (Humphrey Bogart) is shown an odd-looking revolver that has just been used in a murder and questioned if it's a Webley. His response is "Yeah. Webley-Fosbery .45 automatic. Eight shot. Don't make 'em anymore."

Yes, there actually was an automatic revolver—the above-mentioned Webley-Fosbery, designed by British Colonel George Vincent Fosbery, VC (in fact there were actually two such contrivances—the other one a lesser-known American product).

Fosbery, whose military career spanned some 25 years, was also an inveterate firearms tinkerer, coming up with such things as a distinctive "Paradox" rifling system and explosive projectiles. Around the turn of the 20th century he focused his attention on the automatic pistol.

THE FOSBERY CAN GET OFF SHOTS AS FAST AS ANY CONVENTIONAL SEMI-AUTOMATIC, THOUGH THE DYNAMICS ARE SOMEWHAT DIFFERENT.

Remember, this was the dawning of the auto age. Such inventors as Georg Luger, Hugo Borchardt and John Browning were coming to the fore with their ingenious self-loading handguns. Fosbery sought to add his name to the list. Eschewing the more usual frame/slide/magazine concepts, the colonel turned his thoughts to an entirely different style of repeater.

Externally it would look much like the six-shot double-action products then being turned out by Webley & Scott. This superficial resemblance, along with the adoption of the famed Webley "stirrup latch," would be just about the only thing that Fosbery's pistol would have in common with its more prosaic cousin.

Using a cylinder cut with angular channels, à la the style devised by Yankee Elihu Root a half century before, the first Fosbery appeared in 1901 in calibers .445 and .38 Colt Automatic. Guns chambered for the former caliber held six rounds and those for the latter, eight. The frame was divided into two halves. The upper portion fit into rails on the lower and could slide to the rear where it cocked the gun and rotated the cylinder.

The gun was loaded in the usual Webley manner. The stirrup latch was pressed forward with the right-hand thumb, the gun "broken" open

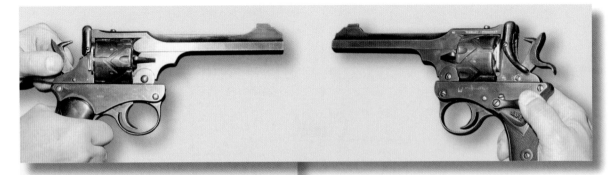

The Fosbery cylinder is removed by simply pushing a top-mounted release button.

The Webley-Fosbery employs the classic stirrup-latch simultaneous ejection system of standard Webley revolvers.

As the Fosbery's cylinder is not linked to the hammer, it revolves by a stud working though the angular milled channels when the top portion of the action moves to the rear.

and cartridges inserted in the chambers. It was then closed. To begin firing, the hammer had to be manually cocked (it was not linked to the cylinder in any manner). When the trigger was pulled and the round discharged, the force of the recoil drove the upper mechanism, consisting of the barrel, cylinder and recoil shield, rearward for approximately three-quarters of an inch. As the cylinder traveled rearward, its machine-cut grooves contacted a protruding stationary stud set into the lower portion of the frame and the cylinder turned half of a chamber revolution. The rearward travel of the upper mechanism stopped against the recoil buffer spring and its travel recocked the hammer. As the recoil energy dissipated and the upper unit began its return travel to forward position, the cylinder rotated through the remaining half chamber position through contact with the lower stud, aligned with the barrel and locked into position, ready for firing.

This all happens in a split second…just as fast, in fact, as a more conventional auto.

Between 1901 and 1902, some modifications were made in the design which basically involved an improvement in the cylinder cuts and cylinder release mechanism.

The Fosbery's safety consisted of a lever at the top of the grip which, when pushed downward, moved the upper part of the frame to the rear, taking the gun out of battery and rendering it inoperable.

Various versions of the Webley-Fosbery were offered, including service and target models. It was found that the exposure of the cylinder grooves to dirt could cause the mechanism to shut down; consequently it was never really considered for general military issue (though apparently some were given to the Royal Naval Air Service during World War I, and some officers opted to carry them unofficially).

Another complaint was that if there was a misfire, simply pulling the trigger or cocking the hammer would not rotate the cylinder to present an unfired round, in the manner of the service Webley Mark VI. This gripe was countered by the observation that the gun was actually an automatic pistol, not a DA revolver and that this clearing problem was endemic to all autos. Too, the sides of the hammer were provided with knurling so it could be easily gripped to pull the top part of the frame to the rear to turn the cylinder and cock the hammer in one facile motion. Actually, I have tried this and find it to be just as fast as recharging a 1911 Government Model or similar auto.

Though the Fosbery failed to achieve government recognition, it became popular with target shooters who particularly appreciated the gun's crisp trigger. Special, long-barreled, adjustable-sighted models were fabricated for this purpose. Crack shot Walter Winans preferred the Webley-Fosbery over any other form of auto. In one exceptional feat of marksmanship, he managed to place 15 out of 18 shots in a 2-inch bull's-eye at 35 feet, rapid fire, offhand.

It was found early on that the British shooting public was less than impressed with the .38 ACP chambering. Very few guns were manufactured in this caliber, making them valuable collectors' pieces today. We were fortunate in obtaining a shootable 1902 Model Fosbery with a 6-inch barrel, non-adjustable sights and hard-rubber grips. Ammo chosen was 265-grain lead Fiocchi Mark II .455 and 265-grain lead handloads.

The gun was first fired offhand to get a feel for the thing. True to form, one is able to crank off six shots as fast as he can work the trigger. The pull was excellent, coming in at a crisp 3½ pounds, and recoil was not unpleasant. The gun does have dynamics unlike any other auto I have ever fired—kind of top heavy. This provided for excellent target reacquisition and good general overall control.

The piece was then fired from a rest at 25 yards. The Fiocchi fodder shot all over the place,

but Jeff John's handloads tightened groups to around 3 inches. Offhand at 7 yards we were able to put all six shots under 2½ inches.

The gun loaded and ejected like a standard Webley Mark VI. While we stoked the chambers one round at a time, back in the 'teens the gun could be provided with a Prideaux device that charged all six cartridges at once—kind of an early speed-loader.

The Webley-Fosbery was fun to shoot, accurate and reliable. Its excellent trigger and good feel make it evident why it was popular with targeteers some 80 years ago and why, in certain conditions, it might not prove to be too bad a combat sidearm.

OUR EVALUATION FOSBERY, BEING A 6-INCH-BARRELED "MILITARY" STYLE, DID NOT EXHIBIT THE ACCURACY THE AUTHOR HAS EXPERIENCED WITH ADJUSTABLE-SIGHTED TARGET MODELS. STILL, AT 25 YARDS THE GUN PERFORMED ADMIRABLY.

25 yds
Webley-Fosbery
.455 Handloads

THE WEBLEY-FOSBERY CHAMBERS THE STANDARD MARK II .455 WEBLEY ROUND (LEFT). BALLISTICS ARE SIMILAR TO BUT SLIGHTLY LESS POTENT THAN THOSE OF A .45 ACP (RIGHT).

Red Nine: C.96 Mauser

This variant of the famed "Broomhandle" was used as a stopgap military sidearm during World War One.

The "Broomhandle" Mauser is perhaps the most stylish auto pistol ever designed. Introduced in 1896, this was the handgun that really legitimized the concept of the self-loader.

True, as soon as the first Browning auto and Luger appeared, the gun was pretty well obsolete, but it just refused to go away and remained in production for some 40 years. The favorite sidearm of Winston Churchill, it was also popular with the militaries of China, Turkey and Persia, among others, though its place of origin, Germany, only adopted it as a secondary arm during the first World War.

In the last decades of the 19th century, the Mauser company had toyed with target pistols, revolvers and a manually operated ring-trigger multi-shot, but development of a true auto pistol was not undertaken until 1894. In less than a year Mauser engineers had come up with a prototype short recoil-operated repeater.

Mauser chose the 7.65mm Borchardt cartridge as a basis for the round of the new pistol. The 7.63 Mauser round was identical in dimension to the round planned for the Borchardt, though its load propelled the 86-grain bullet at 1,400 feet-per-second (fps) velocity—some 300 fps faster than its progenitor.

The C.96 ("Construction" 96), as the gun was called, employed a frontally mounted integral box magazine that held 10 rounds. Ammo was loaded into the magazine by means of a stripper clip. While individual cartridges could be inserted manually against the follower, this was a tedious process and was only recommended for emergency charging.

The grip is circular in cross section, with a rounded, bag-style silhouette. Actually its configuration is not unlike the handles of many European revolvers of the period, and while odd to the American eye, is actually quite comfortable.

The C.96 employed a locked breech, short-recoil system involving a rectangular bolt which operated within a channel housed by a barrel extension integral with the 5½-inch barrel. This assembly was slotted and locked within the pistol's frame. When the gun was fired, the bolt (containing an inertial firing pin), the barrel and extension and the locking piece (which is sited beneath the bolt, affixed to the barrel extension) recoiled slightly, unlocking the bolt and allowing it to move fully to the rear where it cocked the hammer. A recoil spring (also inside the bolt) returned the bolt to battery, stripping a round from the follower/magazine and chambering it.

THE C.96 HAS AN INTEGRAL BOX MAGAZINE AND IS LOADED USING THE PICTURED STRIPPER CLIP.

THE BROOMHANDLE HAS REAR LADDER SIGHTS GRADUATED TO 1,000 METERS. EVEN WITH A SHOULDER STOCK, 1,000 METERS WAS NOT REASONABLE.

When the last round was expended, the follower stopped the bolt from closing, indicating that the Mauser was empty.

Very early Broomhandles had spurred hammers that gave way to round "cone"-shaped models which obscured the sights when down, indicating that the gun was not cocked. In 1899 these cones evolved into large rings, which were altered, five years later, into a smaller, non-obtrusive ring.

While the first guns had milled, recessed frames, for a time they also were made with flat sides. This was considered aesthetically unappealing, so the milling was reintroduced and remained throughout the remainder of the gun's life.

The Mauser's adjustable rear tangent sight was routinely graduated to an optimistic 1,000 meters in 100 meter increments.

The first C.96s had no provisions for shoulder stocks, but this was soon remedied with a wooden stock/holster combo that was carried in a leather harness. The stock slotted into a milled area in the rear of the grip.

In 1912, a new variation of the Broomhandle appeared. Though it looked pretty much like its predecessors, the rifling grooves were reduced from six to four and the twist was also changed. Perhaps the most drastic difference was the fitting of an improved safety, termed by Mauser "NS" or *Neues Sicherung*—"new safety." Now the catch, which was located on the rear, left side of the frame, could only be applied if the gun was cocked. Pistols with this feature bear a distinctive "NS" stamped on the rear of their hammers.

While Mauser was never able to garner any large domestic or foreign military contracts for its C.96 prior to World War I, the gun became very popular with civilians.

During the first World War, German authorities realized that P-08 Luger production was not going to be able to cover all their handgun needs, so they placed an order for 150,000 Broomhandles chambered for 9mm Parabellum. As the larger caliber round's base was the same as that of the 7.63, alteration posed few problems. The first guns looked identical to the .30s, with the exception that the rear sight graduations were reduced to 500 meters. It was soon discovered that 7.63mm ammo was being chambered in these guns by mistake, so an order was placed

DESPITE ITS FRONT-HEAVY APPEARANCE, THE BROOMHANDLE IS PRETTY WELL BALANCED AND A DELIGHT TO SHOOT. AFTER A BREAKING-IN PERIOD, RELIABILITY WAS EXCELLENT; ACCURACY WAS ADEQUATE.

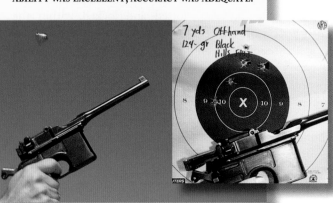

Taking Down the Broomhandle

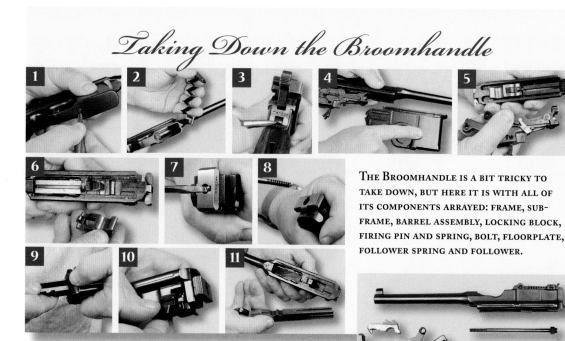

to have the guns' grips carved with a large "9" filled with red paint.

Approximately 130,000 "Red Nines" (as they are called by collectors) were delivered between 1916 and 1918. Guns accepted into service have a military proof on the right side of the barrel flat. Those sold on the postwar civilian market only exhibit the commercial proof.

After Germany's defeat gunmakers were restricted, under the Treaty of Versailles, from producing pistols with calibers larger than 8mm, so Mauser went back to chambering the Broomhandle in .30. In addition, barrel lengths were limited to 4 inches. Many of these Broomhandles had somewhat flattened grip bases. As these pistols were favored by the Russian Communists, they were nicknamed "Bolos," a period diminutive of "Bolshevik."

Mauser continued to manufacture C.96s until 1936, by which time about a million guns had been turned out in numerous versions. They were popular worldwide and used by such disparate militaries as Norway and Siam, along with copies made in China and Spain.

Our evaluation "Red Nine" was a good condition civilian model complete with shoulder stock. Loading a C.96 is fairly simple. Merely pull back on the block until it locks open. Then insert a 10-round clip into the guides in front of the sight and push down on the cartridges until they are secured in the magazine. Removing the clip allows the slide to move forward and chamber a round.

It was decided the gun would be fired from a rest at 25 yards, offhand at 7 yards and with stock affixed at 50 yards. The gun's trigger had about ⅜-inch takeup but broke at a clean 3½ pounds. While the gun failed to go completely into battery for the first few rounds, after a bit of shooting it functioned perfectly. From a rest, 25-yard groups ran some 4 inches, an average that was repeated when firing the gun standing with the shoulder stock. Actually the gun shouldered pretty well despite the diminutive butt, and one needed to hold one's hand under the magazine for proper support.

Overall the Broomhandle is one of the great romantic handguns of all time. Aesthetically it is virtually unsurpassed and design-wise it was not a bad effort for the period.

CLASSIC TEST

The U.S. Military's first general-issue

double-action revolver was an interesting

mix of strengths and weaknesses.

Many collectors and shooters now consider Colt's first swing-out cylinder double-action—the .38 New Model Army and Navy revolver—to be something of a failure. But is this a fair evaluation? No less a firearms enthusiast than Theodore Roosevelt carried a Model 1889 Colt Navy revolver (that had been salvaged from the sunken battleship U.S.S. Maine) during his "crowded hour" at San Juan Hill in the Spanish-American War and managed to dispatch a Spanish soldier whom he said "crumpled like a jackrabbit."

On the other hand, many soldiers were only too happy to trade in their DA .38s for older Colt Single Actions. And during the Moro uprising in the Philippines, the .38 Colt cartridge was deemed insufficient in stopping

THE COLT NEW ARMY MODEL REVOLVER WAS A STAPLE DURING THE SPANISH-AMERICAN WAR, THOUGH NOT ALWAYS A FIRST CHOICE.

fanatical warriors. As a result, the .45 caliber (in Single-Action Armies and Colt New Service revolvers) was readopted and this change culminated in the acceptance of the famed .45 ACP Government Model auto in 1911.

By the last quarter of the 19th century most of Europe had moved toward the double-action revolver, and the U.S. decided to follow suit. Instead of adapting one of the fine foreign systems—such as the British Webley or French Chamelot-Delvign—it was decided to "buy American," and Ordnance officials opted for a new DA designed by Colt. Never mind that the earlier Colt Models 1877 and 1878 double-actions were considered somewhat lacking in the reliability department (especially when compared to some of the foreign designs), the new Colt offering was sleek, felt good in the hand and offered the novelty of a swing-out cylinder for loading and ejecting.

First in line was the Model 1889 Navy

Groups with the black powder handloads were disappointing. The resulting keyholes are attributable to undersized bullets and underpowered loads. Factory ammo fared much, much better.

and while they were reasonably well received, some deficiencies were noted, including the cylinder locking system. This led to a litany of changes wherein generally minor alterations accounted for several models of the basic gun spaced out between 1892 and 1903. While the military stayed with the original .38 caliber, civilian versions in .41 were also available.

The .38 round itself sported a 150-grain bullet moving out at 770 fps to produce a muzzle energy of 195 ft-lbs. Compare this to the previous .45 Colt round, which pushed its 255-grain pellet out at 810 fps with a ME of around 400 ft-lbs., and it is obvious that the military took a major step backward in the puissance department.

Still, it was a handsome revolver—very modern-looking and efficient from a loading and unloading standpoint. It was a good, natural pointer, and while the sights were rudimentary—involving a blade front and notch-in-the-topstrap rear—at least they were no worse than those of the Colt SAA.

Frankly, from an aesthetic and historical standpoint, I have always had a penchant for the New Model Army and Navy. In fact, I have a couple of them in my own collection, one of which I pulled out of mothballs for this evaluation.

My gun is, in fact, a Model 1894 Army revolver in just about 95 percent condition. Like its mates, it sports a beautiful, high-luster blue, a hammer with polished sides and walnut grips emblazoned with the date "1898" and the inspectors' initials of Rinaldo A. Carr and Daniel M. Taylor.

Functioning was perfect and the bore like

Revolver, chambered for .38 "Long" Colt. The gun (in military guise) was blued, had a six-inch barrel and hard rubber grips. Civilian versions were also offered with shorter 4½-inch barrels, nickel-plated finishes, etc.

The Navy purchased a total of 5,000 guns,

a mirror. For a shooter, one really couldn't do much better.

Chosen ammunition included some .38 Colt black powder handloads and a few rounds of some now-out-of-print smokeless Remington ammo.

As noted earlier, the gun felt very good in the hand. The cylinder can be easily opened by simply pulling the latch on the left side of the frame behind the recoil shield to the rear. Cartridges are then loaded into the chambers and the cylinder closed. To eject, one merely opens the cylinder and pushes back on a centrally-mounted rod which activates a star extractor. As the gun has an rebounding-hammer setup, there is no half-cock notch.

I tried a few cylinders-full of both types of ammo with interesting results. Rested, single-action 25-yard spreads with the older Remington ammo came in at around 3 inches and 7-yard DA strings ran about the same. The handloads fared much worse, and I experienced serious keyholing. I can only assume that the bullets were far too undersized. Still, at least they stayed on the paper. The SA trigger pull measured a very crisp but hefty 7 pounds, and the DA pull was a long, smooth 13 pounds. Neither were particularly conducive to great accuracy, but still the Colt actually performed pretty well. Recoil wasn't particularly impressive, as one might expect from such a marginal load.

There is no question that the Colt New Model Army and Navy revolver is a beautifully made gun. While it is tempting to dismiss the double-action system as somewhat lacking, I must admit that in seeing and handling scores of these six-shooters over the years, I have never seen one in reasonably good shape with a defective mechanism. Would I feel comfortable carrying one in combat? Probably not. The .38 LC round is not one to inspire confidence. Still, T.R. had no trouble dealing with an adversary with his, and there are accounts by other officers who praise the gun as well. Perhaps I'm just too hidebound and steeped in the mystique of the .45.

TO OPEN THE ACTION ON THE NEW MODEL SERIES, PUSH BACK ON A REAR-MOUNTED LATCH TO SWING THE CYLINDER OUT TO THE LEFT.

LOADING THE CYLINDER IS AS SIMPLE AS PLACING INDIVIDUAL CARTRIDGES IN THEIR CHAMBERS. EJECTION IS EFFECTED BY PUSHING BACK ON THE CENTRALLY-MOUNTED CYLINDER ROD (ABOVE).

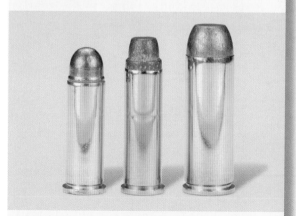

THE .38 COLT (LEFT, NEXT TO A .38 SPECIAL AND .45 COLT) WASN'T EXACTLY A BARNBURNER IN THE STOPPING-POWER DEPARTMENT. STILL, IT REMAINED IN SERVICE FOR SOME 20 YEARS.

Models 1903 and 1908

were among the most popular carry pistols ever made.

Without question, from numbers made and sold, longevity, and the widespread distribution of the Colt Model M, it ranks as one of the most successful autos of its type ever designed. The gun's reliability, sleek lines and seven-round capacity made it a favorite of generals, gangsters, private dicks, police forces (foreign and domestic) and ordinary citizens.

Actually, the Model M series is comprised of two models (with some sub-variations): the Model 1903 in .32 ACP and the Model 1908 in .380 ACP. But I'm getting ahead of myself.

It should come as no surprise that such a handy little piece of machinery originated in the mind of John M. Browning. As evidenced by the pistol's "1903" designation, it

THE COLT MODEL M WAS ONE OF THE MOST POPULAR AUTO PISTOLS EVER DESIGNED. DURING WORLD WAR II IT WAS DRAFTED INTO U.S. SERVICE AND ISSUED TO SUPPORT TROOPS AND GENERAL OFFICERS. PICTURED IS A PARKERIZED GI-ISSUE 1903, GENERAL OFFICER'S HOLSTER AND BELT RIG, AND JACKET.

first appeared in that year, manufactured by Colt who, according to an agreement with Browning, would market the guns in the U.S. Fabrique Nationale in Belgium was authorized to make and sell Browning's wares in Europe.

The 1903 was chambered for .32 ACP. Its relatively small size (6¾ x 4 x 1¹⁄₁₀ inches), light weight (23 ounces) and sleek, hammerless silhouette (there was also a clunkier 1903 hammer pocket pistol produced at the same time) made it a natural for carry in a shoulder holster, or coat or trouser pocket. It featured both a grip and manual safety—the latter also doubling as a slide hold-open. Sights were pretty rudimentary, consisting of a small blade front and narrow U-notch rear, which was later changed to a square notch. Finish was originally blue, though nickel, sliver and even gold plating were offered in fairly short order. Of course, the guns could be had with engraving on special order, and the standard checkered hard rubber grips could be replaced with walnut, pearl and ivory of varying fanciness, should the purchaser so

THE EVALUATION 1903 WAS RELIABLE AND EASY TO SHOOT WITH ALL AMMUNITION TRIED. RECOIL WAS SHARPER THAN EXPECTED, BUT NOT PROHIBITIVE.

THE AUTHOR'S MODEL M PROVED TO BE QUITE ACCURATE FROM A REST, AS ATTESTED BY THIS 15-YARD RESTED GROUP. THE MOST ACCURATE AMMO WAS SPEER'S 60-GRAIN JHP.

THE MODEL M'S MAGAZINE HELD SEVEN ROUNDS, AND IS RELEASED BY MEANS OF A HEEL MOUNTED BUTTON.

specify. Other extras included such things as lanyard loops and belt clips.

Originally, the Model M had a 4-inch barrel and separate barrel bushing, but after about 72,000 units had been produced, it was altered to a 3¾-inch barrel and bushings disappeared around serial number 105,000. A few guns in the 104,000 range were also apparently fitted with magazine safeties. In 1908 the .380 Model M appeared with little to differentiate it from its predecessor, except chambering.

With the onset of World War II, the Model M was mobilized. Several thousand were purchased by Great Britain, and the United States drafted large quantities, each marked "U.S. Property" on its frame. Both .32s and .380s saw service. Finishes were either blue or parkerized, and grips were normally checkered walnut inset with silver Colt medallions.

Model Ms were issued to support troops and general officers. George S. Patton included both variations of the Model M in his personal arsenal, the grips emblazoned with distinctive general's stars. Generals were also given beautiful holster sets with their Model Ms. They were made by Hickock, were of brown leather and featured an adjustable belt, holster with snap loop and dual magazine pouch. The outfit's gold-plated two-piece buckle featured the U.S. National Emblem in high relief. Actually, general officers continued to be given Colt Pockets for a number of years following WWII. The main difference between theirs and earlier ones was that black leather was substituted for brown, in keeping with the Army's post-war changeover.

By the time the Model M was phased out of production in 1945, some 747,585 1903s and 138,009 1908s had been manufactured by Colt, making it the most widely produced auto pistol in the firm's venerable history.

Stripping a Model M (later non-barrel bushing version) is simple. First remove the magazine and inspect the chamber to ensure the gun is unloaded. Then draw the slide rearward against the recoil spring pressure, until the arrowed line inscribed on the right side of the slide just below the muzzle is aligned with the forward edge off the frame. Rotate the barrel 180 degrees counterclockwise and run the slide forward of the frame. The barrel can then be removed rearward, out of the slide, along with the recoil spring. Reassemble in the reverse order.

As noted, the Model M has a grip safety and small safety catch on the rear, left side of the frame. The magazine release is a simple heel-mounted button that must be pushed back to drop the mag. While I have heard some writers complain that the safety and mag release were just too fiddly for smooth operation, I have never found them to be so. To be sure, I don't have particularly large hands, but still, I would think that with a little practice, even the most ham-fisted of us could manage. Al Capone was not the most dainty of humans, and he seemed to have no trouble with his Colt Pocket.

I have two 1903s, one a British issue piece replete with broad-arrow proofmarks, black paint finish and all the signs of pretty hard use. My other Pocket is an almost 98 percent parkerized U.S.-issue piece, and it was this latter gun I chose to feature here, figuring it would provide the best example of how the model would perform.

Selected ammo included 90-grain Blazer FMJs and Speer 60-grain JHPs. The gun was fired from a rest at 15 yards and offhand at 7 yards. Functioning was perfect with both loads. The gun barked a tad, and recoil was a bit stouter than I have come to expect with a .32—but by no means off-putting. The best groups from a rest came in at just under 2 inches, while rapid-fire, 7 yarders spread out to about 3 inches. To be sure, the small square notch rear sight was not wonderful for rapid target acquisition, but one must remember that this is essentially a close-range defense gun, and more likely than not would have be used for quick snap shots.

By far the .32 was the most popular of the Model Ms, and it's easy to see why. If you need a .380, you might as well move up to a .38 or 9mm. The .32 is, to me, the classic pocket gun caliber, and the 1903 Colt the quintessential pocket gun.

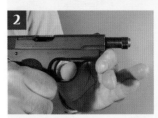

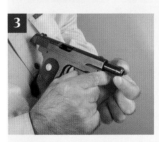

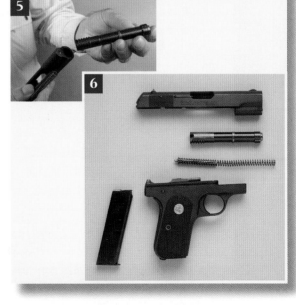

To fieldstrip the Model M, first remove the magazine and ensure the gun is unloaded. (1) Locate the arrow on the front of the slide (2) and move the slide backward to where the line behind the arrow matches up with the front of the slide. (3) Turn the barrel 180 degrees (4) and move the slide forward off the frame. (5) Remove barrel recoil spring and guide. (6) The gun is now taken down into its basic components. Reassemble in reverse order.

*This stopgap revolver turned out to be
a reliable, if moderately used, substitute standard
sidearm during two world wars.*

By the time the United States entered World War I in 1917, the Model 1911 Government Model auto pistol had been our official sidearm for some six years.

Unfortunately, Uncle Sam had not produced enough of them to supply the vast numbers of doughboys that he planned to send to France, so it was decided in 1916 that development begin on a method of altering existing arms to handle the .45 ACP cartridge. Initial experimentation was undertaken by Smith & Wesson, which modified its Second Model Hand Ejector revolver to chamber the rimless auto round. It achieved this by altering the cylinder to accept the ammunition, which was snapped into a pair of three-round spring-steel "half-moon" clips to facilitate loading and ejection. The system worked quite well and was also applied to the popular Colt New Service revolver.

The New Service, which was initially cataloged in 1898, was a large-frame, robust sixgun that proved to be Colt's first really reliable double-action. It saw considerable civilian use, was accepted by the Canadian North West Mounted Police in 1905 and, in .45 Long Colt, was carried by the U.S. Military as early as 1909 when, during the Philippine Campaign, the .38s then being issued were found lacking in stopping power against Moro tribesmen. At the outset of the Great War, the British—short on just about every kind of small arm—also ordered a large quantity of them in .455.

From the time of its introduction until its demise in 1944, Colt turned out some 355,000 New Service revolvers. As well as the chamberings mentioned above, at various times during its lifespan the gun could also be had in .38 Colt (Long and Short), .38 Special, .357 Magnum, .38-40, .38-44, .44-40, .44 Special, .44 Russian, .450, .455 and .476. Barrel lengths ranged from 2 to 7½ inches. There were special target models with adjustable sights (the standard gun had a simple blade front sight and notch-in-topstrap rear), versions embellished with fancy grips, engraving, gold-and-silver decoration and even bobbed carry versions.

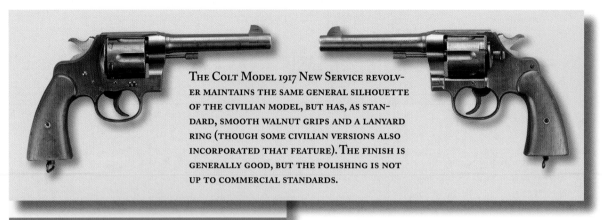

THE COLT MODEL 1917 NEW SERVICE REVOLVER MAINTAINS THE SAME GENERAL SILHOUETTE OF THE CIVILIAN MODEL, BUT HAS, AS STANDARD, SMOOTH WALNUT GRIPS AND A LANYARD RING (THOUGH SOME CIVILIAN VERSIONS ALSO INCORPORATED THAT FEATURE). THE FINISH IS GENERALLY GOOD, BUT THE POLISHING IS NOT UP TO COMMERCIAL STANDARDS.

DESPITE ITS SIZE, THE NEW SERVICE FITS WELL IN THE HAND AND IS AN EXCELLENT, RELIABLE SHOOTER. INSET: GROUPS WITH THE '17 NEW SERVICE WERE CERTAINLY MILITARY-GRADE-ACCEPTABLE. COMMERCIAL TARGET VERSIONS OF THIS GUN WERE HIGHLY REGARDED BY MARKSMEN.

25 YDS
.45 ACP 230 GR. B.E.B.
WINCHESTER

made with straight chambers, but later guns had stepped cylinders so that, in a pinch, .45s could be loaded without the clips. If loaded naked, the ACP cases could not be engaged by the star extractor, so it was necessary to poke them out one at a time with some sort of rod.

With the exception of the modified cylinder, the Model 1917 New Service was pretty close to the regular over-the-counter factory product, and it came standard with smooth walnut grips and a lanyard ring at the base of the butt. The finish was blued, though the gun was not polished as highly as the civilian model. Barrel length was 5½ inches, and the sights were the usual nonadjustable style. As well as the standard Colt legend on the top of the barrel, the '17 was stamped "UNITED STATES PROPERTY" on the underside of the barrel and "U.S./ARMY/MODEL/1917" in front of the lanyard ring.

While the New Service was able to take advantage of some accessories already in the military pipeline (lanyards, pistol belts, cleaning gear), some specific items had to be developed. A russet leather holster, similar to the style used with the older Colt .38 Army & Navy, was added to the inventory, as was a three-pouch canvas ammunition carrier that held six three-round half-moon clips full of ammo.

The New Service was not a small revolver, weighing in at 40 ounces (4½-inch barrel), though it was well balanced with a comfortable grip and pleasant, positive double-action. The cylinder latch, a portion of which also acted as a recoil shield, was pulled to the rear to free the cylinder (unlike the S&W Hand Ejector, which employed a latch that had to be pushed forward). Once the cylinder was swung out, spent cases were removed by pushing back on a stout ejector rod. The first 50,000 1917s were

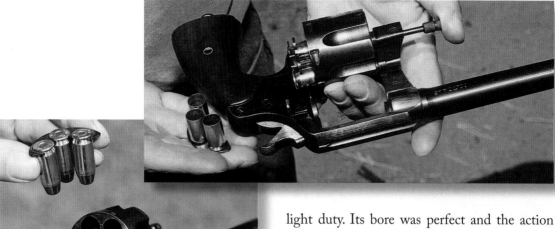

MODEL 1917 REVOLVERS (BOTH SMITH & WESSON AND COLT) WERE LOADED WITH THE AID OF HALF-MOON CLIPS. THESE ALLOWED THE RIMLESS ROUNDS TO BE LOADED FASTER AND BE EXTRACTED PROPERLY.

While the 1917 Colts and Smiths were never issued in the numbers of the Government Model, a goodly quantity made it to the trenches, where they were well regarded. In fact, some of the veteran officers actually preferred the revolvers to the newfangled auto.

As the war drew to a close in 1918, orders for the Colt were stopped, though some 151,700 had been produced. After the conflict, all of the Colts and Smiths were pulled from service and put into storage. With the onset of World War II, however, they were again issued to British and American units. Apparently the British reserved them for the Home Guard, though some 1917s did see actual service in Europe and the Pacific with the U.S. Army and Marines.

Our evaluation 1917 was a very clean New Service, exhibiting about 90 percent of the original finish. My guess is that the gun was probably never issued, or if it was, it certainly saw

light duty. Its bore was perfect and the action tight and crisp. The single-action trigger pull came in at a very military 6½ pounds, while the DA broke at just under 15 pounds. Admittedly these are not exactly target-grade, but that's precisely the way the Army wanted it in order to prevent accidental discharges and such. We found that once one got used to them, even the double-action was perfectly manageable. This was abetted, to a large degree, by the excellent grip and generous trigger configuration.

The small notch rear sight was not exactly ideal for combat use, and we found target reacquisition to be a tad dicey. Still, the gun turned in respectable 3½ to 4-inch, 25-yard rested groups using 230-grain Winchester .45 ACP. The half-moon clips worked perfectly and facilitated both charging and ejection. One could consider them a sort of early speed-loading device and, in fact, similar appliances are currently being offered for just such a purpose. Functioning was perfect and 7-yard DA spreads not too bad—certainly combat-worthy.

While I always have been a big fan of the 1911, were I issued a 1917 New Service, I would not feel at a particular disadvantage during a trench raid or sojourn in no-man's land.

Throughout its career, the New Service proved to be a rugged, no-nonsense bit of hardware. I have personally owned several over the years in various configurations and have had no experience to the contrary. It can certainly hold its own with many of the guns currently on the market, especially in the area of versatility. In short, it's a fine revolver and one that is worthy of a regular reexamination.

CLASSIC TEST

What this .380 Italian service pistol lacked in power,

it more than made up for in reliability.

W orld War II was one of the last conflicts where pocket pistols were considered serious military sidearms. To be fair, Germany's primary handguns were the 9mm P.38 and Luger, but there were also scads of .32s and .380s (and even some .25s) being carried. Walthers, Mausers, CZs and MABs all could be seen dangling from officers' waistbelts. Even the Allies were not immune to this trend, and the U.S., for instance, issued Colt Pocket autos to generals and specialized troops, and even fielded some Colt Vest Pocket .25s. Italy carried the fashion one step further and adopted a .380 as its primary handgun. It was one of the best-designed pistols of the war, but it was still a .380, or as the Italians called it, "9mm Corto."

THE BERETTA MODEL 34 WAS A POPULAR WAR TROPHY WITH RETURNING GIs. WHILE IT WAS OFFICIAL ITALIAN ISSUE, SOME WERE ALSO USED BY THE WEHRMACHT.

The Beretta Model 1934 (there was also a Model 35 in 7.62mm) was a member of a long line of top-notch autos (Models 1915, 1919, 1923 and 1931). Like its predecessors, it was a small blowback. Primary orders came from the Italian Army, followed by Air Force purchases. The gun became so popular it was eventually declared standard issue, though a number of older Italian handguns, such as the Bodeo revolvers and Model 1910 Glisenti auto, were issued to Mussolini's Fascist forces.

When Italy left the war, a number of Model 34s and 35s were also carried by German officers. In fact, the gun I am using for this evaluation came in a German marked holster.

The Model 34 was simply a great gun. Exhibiting typical Beretta quality (even in late war versions), it was easy to operate, not difficult to take down and reliable in the extreme. Grips were black plastic emblazoned with the Pietro Beretta (PB) monogram. Finish was a

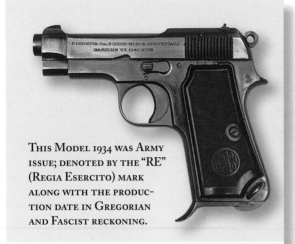

THIS MODEL 1934 WAS ARMY ISSUE; DENOTED BY THE "RE" (REGIA ESERCITO) MARK ALONG WITH THE PRODUCTION DATE IN GREGORIAN AND FASCIST RECKONING.

THE MODEL 1934'S SAFETY IS A SMALL LEVER THAT MUST BE ROTATED 180 DEGREES FORWARD BEFORE THE PISTOL CAN BE FIRED.

LIKE MANY OTHER EUROPEAN (AND SOME AMERICAN) AUTOS OF THE PERIOD, THE MODEL 1934 HAS A HEEL-MOUNTED SAFETY CATCH. THIS IS NOT AS EASY TO MANIPULATE AS A FRAME BUTTON, BUT IS VERY POSITIVE.

THE MAGAZINE HOLDS SEVEN ROUNDS. IT HAS OPEN SIDES SO ONE CAN EASILY DETERMINE HOW MANY CARTRIDGES HAVE BEEN LOADED. SOME EXPERTS FEEL THIS FEATURE ALLOWS DIRT AND DEBRIS IN.

combination of a blued frame and plum-colored slide. The safety, which also served as a slide hold-open, was located on the left side of the frame, where it could easily be manipulated with the thumb of the right hand.

I've heard some people complain that rotating the lever 180 degrees to put the gun on and off "safe" is a bit cumbersome, but I must admit I have never found it so.

Like so many European pistols of the time, the magazine had a heel release. When the final round was expended the slide locked open and closed when the magazine was removed. The gun featured an external hammer. Sights involved a simple blade milled out of the top of the forward portion of the slide, and a notch rear that could be drift-adjusted for windage. Capacity was seven rounds in the magazine, plus one in the chamber—so while puissance was somewhat lacking in the .380 round, at least overall firepower was not.

Markings on the gun are interesting, and just a little bit different. The left side of the slide exhibits the Beretta address, model and date of manufacture—in the Gregorian calendar in Arabic numerals, and the Fascist calendar, which started in 1922, in Roman numerals. Thus my test piece is dated both "1940" and "XVIII." Military pistols are also stamped either "RE" for *Regia Esercito* (Royal Army), "RA" for *Regia Aeronautica* (Royal Air Force) or "RM" for *Regia Marina* (Royal Navy.)

Barrel length on the 1934 is 3⅜ inches, overall length is 6 inches and it weighs some 24 ounces.

The M34 and M35 proved to be very popular with returning GIs, and even though thousands were brought back to the States as war trophies, Beretta recognized that there was still a market for this popular little pistol and continued making it for civilians until 1958.

Stripping the Beretta 34/35 is rela-

THE BERETTA 34 WAS FAIRLY ACCURATE AT CLOSE RANGE. AT 25 YARDS THE PISTOL PRODUCED GROUPS WITHIN THREE INCHES WHEN FIRED FROM A REST.

tively simple. First remove the magazine and ensure the gun is unloaded. Now lock back the slide with the safety lever and tap on the muzzle to free the barrel from the frame. Remove the slide forward off the frame and pull out the recoil spring and spring guide. Reassemble in reverse order.

My evaluation 34 was in excellent condition, exhibiting little use and only marginal blue wear. The bore was perfect and the trigger a crisp 5¼ pounds. After a little checking, wiping and oiling, it was ready to take to the range. It might be noted that in all probability, this was the first time the gun had been fired since the war.

Ammo chosen was Black Hills 95-grain FMJ, as it pretty closely approximates the Italian service load. The magazine was charged with seven rounds, a cartridge chambered and the trigger pulled. Nothing. Another round was chambered. Nothing again. I checked the primers, and they had been barely dimpled. The mag was removed, the slide pulled back and a punch used to push on the rear of the firing pin. It was, to say the least, a tad on the stiff side.

When pushed all the way forward, the pin protruded far enough to discharge a round, so it was determined that in all probability some fugitive dried oil or grease was inhibiting its proper forward travel. After putting a few drops of light oil in the rear of the pin and working it back and forth a few times, the gun was reloaded and tried again. Success!

I ran through a couple of magazines full of ammo just to make sure all was in good order, and then tried for accuracy. From a rest at 25 yards, it kept most of its rounds in sub 3-inch groups about four inches above point of aim. Not too bad for a pocket piece.

Recoil was not unpleasant, and it proved to be a lot of fun to shoot. Targets of opportunity at varying closer ranges were handily picked off, exhibiting more than adequate combat accuracy.

While I admit the Beretta 34 would not be my first choice for a service pistol, I'll also admit it certainly has a presence and considerable amount of jaunty élan—just like the Italians who first used it.

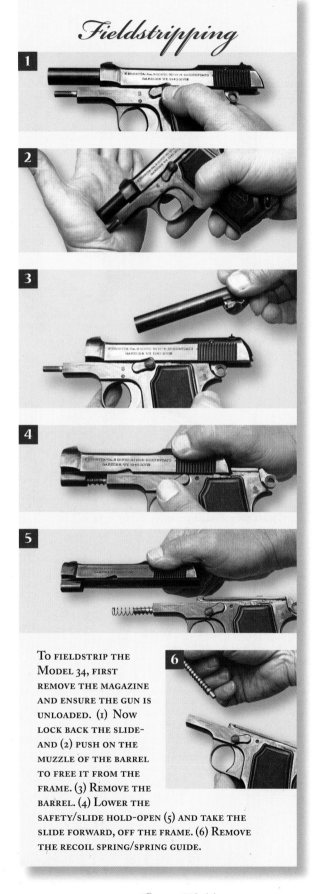

Fieldstripping

TO FIELDSTRIP THE MODEL 34, FIRST REMOVE THE MAGAZINE AND ENSURE THE GUN IS UNLOADED. (1) NOW LOCK BACK THE SLIDE- AND (2) PUSH ON THE MUZZLE OF THE BARREL TO FREE IT FROM THE FRAME. (3) REMOVE THE BARREL. (4) LOWER THE SAFETY/SLIDE HOLD-OPEN (5) AND TAKE THE SLIDE FORWARD, OFF THE FRAME. (6) REMOVE THE RECOIL SPRING/SPRING GUIDE.

Browning Hi-Power

*Without question, this 14-shot autopistol is the most
successful handgun of its type ever devised.*

Given a number of monikers throughout its long life—"GP," "Hi-Power," "P-35," "Pistole 640(b)," etc.—there's no question that the Hi-Power is the most successful autopistol ever devised, and one that has seen service throughout the world with military and police forces as well as being a highly popular civilian sidearm. Supposedly, the Hi-Power got its start at the behest of the French government, which put in a requirement to Fabrique Nationale in Herstal, Belgium, for a large-capacity service handgun. This tale may or may not be apocryphal, but the fact remains that by the mid-1930s the perfected product appeared.

Browning had been working on the gun's basic design, but when he died, the task was taken up by FN designer Dieudonne Saive, who incorporated some of Browning's concepts and added a few of his own. Saive would later gain even more fame as the designer of the superb FN-FAL military rifle.

The challenge of producing a workable, large-capacity autopistol was one that had

THE HI-POWER AUTO WAS ONE OF FEW GUNS FIELDED BY BOTH SIDES DURING WORLD WAR II. THE GERMAN-MADE GUNS WERE DESIGNATED PISTOLE 640(B) AND THE ALLIED, INGLIS AUTOS AS NO. 1 AND NO. 2 (PICTURED).

plagued inventors for years. One early solution appeared in WWI, where 25-round trench magazines were developed for the Colt 1911. The problem was, they stuck way out of the gun's butt and really didn't feed well. Other attempts included a curious, Italian chain-drive 20-shot pistol and various attempts at stretching existing mags.

Saive finally solved the problem with a rugged, eminently workable double-stack magazine that could hold 13 rounds of 9mm Parabellum without radically altering the gun's shape. Naturally, the grip would have to be a little thicker, but not so much that it would affect the overall handling of the piece. The mag was mated to a version of Browning's Model 1911 auto, which incorporated some interesting new innovations. Instead of the Government Model's swinging-link arrangement, the new pistol employed an ingenious cam lug. Thus the 1911's barrel bushing could be eliminated, and fieldstripping would be greatly simplified. Too, the earlier stirrup-style trigger connection was jettisoned in favor of a pivoting type that employed a transfer bar in the slide. While the latter worked just fine, it was not as sensitive as the earlier setup and thus was not particularly responsive for target work—though the gun

THE AUTHOR'S BEST THREE-INCH, 25-YARD RESTED GROUPS WITH HIS INGLIS HI-POWER WERE FIRED WITH FEDERAL 115-GRAIN FMJs.

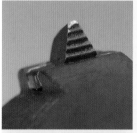

SIGHTS ON THE PISTOL WERE BASIC BUT ADEQUATE AND INVOLVED A SIMPLE NOTCH REAR (TOP) AND SQUARE BLADE FRONT (BELOW). SOME MODELS WERE EQUIPPED WITH 500-METER TANGENT REARS AND WERE NOTCHED TO TAKE SHOULDER STOCKS.

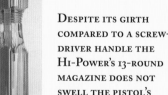

DESPITE ITS GIRTH COMPARED TO A SCREWDRIVER HANDLE THE HI-POWER'S 13-ROUND MAGAZINE DOES NOT SWELL THE PISTOL'S GRIP ALL THAT MUCH.

was designed as a service pistol anyway, and this small complaint hardly mattered.

Controls on the new auto were similar to those of the Government Model and involved a slide stop and safety sited on the left side of the frame. The magazine release was a 1911-style button on the left, just behind the lower portion of the triggerguard. The gun was also equipped with a magazine safety.

The new arm was ready for production in 1935 and was immediately adopted by the Belgian military as the P-35. Also called Pistolet Automatique Modele a Grand Puissance (Hi-Power), this was the name that stuck. Despite the wide magazine, the grip was very comfortable in the hand. The barrel measured five inches, overall length of the gun was 7¾ inches, and it weighed some two pounds, three ounces—about ideal for a service pistol.

Early Belgian military autos featured nifty tang sights graduated to a very optimistic 500 meters, but they were set up to be attached to a combination shoulder stock/holster so at least there was some chance of hitting targets at an extend range.

In very short order other countries such as Estonia, Lithuania and Peru put in bids for Hi-Powers, but the Germans were soon to nullify these contracts in the form of WWII. When the Nazis invaded Belgium and took over the FN plant, they were more than pleased to accept the P-35 into their own service and soon began producing the pistol as the Pistole 640(b). While the general finish was not as good as those on the pre-war Belgian models, quality was still very high—especially early in the war—and the Hi-Power was put into front-line service. Some 300,000 were made for Hitler's effort. Guns of this period generally exhibit the acceptance *Waffenamt* marks WaA103 or WaA140.

Apparently, the British made a few prototype Hi-Powers during the conflict, but it was left to the John Inglis Company of Toronto, Canada, to put the gun in the hands of the Allies. Inglis had acquired blueprints for the auto in 1942 and by 1944 was turning them out at a pretty good clip. Versions included guns with both tangent and regular notch sights. Many were manufactured for the Chinese, whose guns exhibited a "CH" in the serial number.

As well, Inglis-made Hi-Powers were used by British and Canadian Airborne troops and Commandos, as well as anyone who could get his hands on one, the gun being a considerable improvement over the No. 2 Mk 1 Enfield revolver. Inglis autos used by the Brits and Canadians had a "T" in their serial numbers. A Parkerized finish was standard.

There were several Inglis variants. The No. 1 Mk 1 had an adjustable sight and shoulder stock, the No. 1 Mk 1* was the same as the No. 1 Mk 1 but had an improved ejector and barrel cam lugs, the No. 2 Mk 1 had a fixed sight and no stock provision, and the No. 2 Mk 1* had a fixed sight, no stock and the improvements of the No. 1 Mk 1*. While the British had a number of Hi-Powers in inventory, the gun would not be officially adopted as standard issue until 1954.

After the war, FN resumed production of the Grande Puissance, and as well as selling them commercially (very successfully, I might add), managed to secure contracts from more than 50 other countries for the pistol. While most were made in Belgium, some, such as those issued by Argentina, were produced indigenously.

Fieldstripping a Hi-Power is simple. First remove the magazine and ensure the gun is unloaded. Pull back the slide and lock it to the rear by moving the safety catch upward to catch in the takedown notch. Push out on the slide-stop pin from the right side of the frame, and remove the stop from the left side of the pistol. Release the safety from the takedown notch while securely holding onto the slide, and allow the slide to move forward off the frame. Take the recoil spring and guide from the slide,

followed by the barrel. To reassemble the Hi-Power simply follow the directions in reverse order.

My evaluation Hi-Power was an almost-mint Inglis No. 2 Mk 1* (I might advise against shooting the No. 1 Mk 1 and the No. 2 Mk 1 as their rounded cam-slot lugs did have a tendency to break). The gun was in very nice condition and amazingly still had the Canadian ID decal on the front of the gripstrap. Grip panels were made of black checkered plastic.

Chosen 9mm ammunition was Black Hills' 124-grain FMJ and Federal's 115-grain JHP. To be fair, this was not the first time I shot a Hi-Power, or even an Inglis Hi-Power, but there is always an element of rediscovery when I haven't fired a particular arm for a time, and such was the case with the Inglis.

First off, the trigger, which dropped at 6 pounds after a small amount of take-up, was much more agreeable than I remembered. The wide grip seemed to distribute shock well, and recoil was relatively light. Of course, functioning was perfect, and average 25-yard rested groups of 3 inches were just fine for a military gun. Best groups were produced with the Federal ammo. Perhaps my only criticism of the piece is the rather skimpy safety catch that can be a bit difficult to access in a hurry. Rapid-fire, offhand combat groups at 5 yards were deadly accurate and great in number, with none falling outside the black.

There was not a hitch or glitch in shooting more than 150 rounds. The gun certainly lived up to its reputation. Hi-Powers are still sold commercially and many good surplus guns can still be found on the market. I'll go out on a limb and suggest that if you could only own one handgun, the Hi-Power would certainly be a very good choice.

.577 Howdah

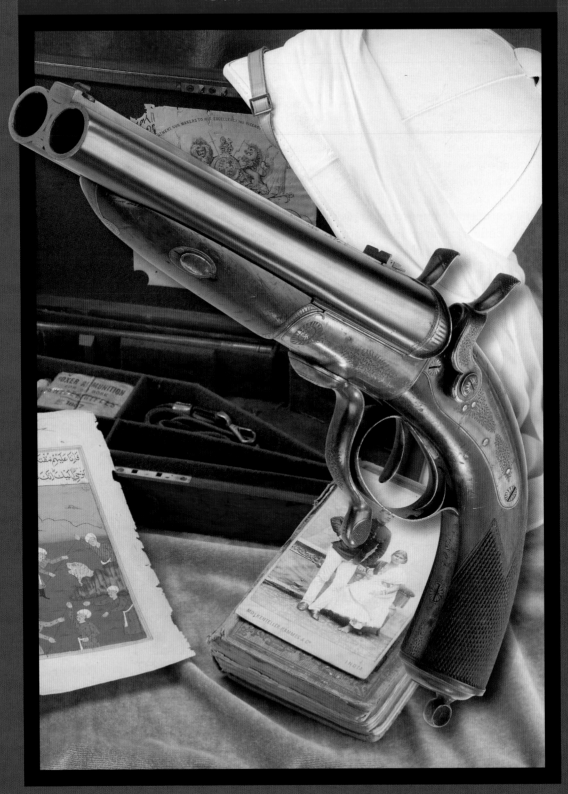

CLASSIC TEST

This double-barreled behemoth was intended as a last ditch, short-range defense against tigers.

The concept of coming within inches of a Bengal tiger in the wild is something that I can only slightly imagine. It is the sort of thing nightmares are made of. Consider, then, that in the middle of the 19th century hunters were doing this on a regular basis—fielding nothing more than large-bore, single- or double-shot black powder arms to bring down one of nature's most formidable predators. Unquestionably, because of the hunting techniques of the period whereby one or more hunters would be carried on the back of an elephant in a secure platform called a howdah, odds were slanted heavily on the side of the pursuer. The practice was excellently described by George Trevelyan in his 1864 collection of stories *The Competition Wallah*.

"The howdah consists of a box of wood and wickerwork, open at top, with sides in front for the Sahib, and a remarkably uncomfortable one behind for the attendant. On either side of the sportsman rest his firearms; a double-barreled rifle and two smoothbores loaded with ball, and one gun with a couple of charges of 'No. 4,' or 'B.B.,' shot for partridge and jungle fowl. As most of the firing consists of snap-

shots within 50 yards, a good smooth-bore is every whit as effective as a grooved barrel. In a little partition in the front of the howdah the ammunition lies ready to hand."

Trevelyan recalled his encounter with a "royal Nepaul tiger" which had been located in the brush not 10 yards away. "Quick as thought came the report of all our rifles, and more than one red spot appeared on his tawny flank. With a roar, a flash of his tail, and one tremendous bound, he was among us. I have a very dim recollection of what followed. Bullets were whizzing all around, Tom firing over my shoulder, and Benson into my howdah; the tiger at one time on the head of Mildred's elephant, at another between the legs of mine; our beasts trumpeting, and plunging, and rolling; the rank and file scampering away in ungovernable terror. At the end of what seemed 10 minutes, and was perhaps 90 seconds, the tiger lay dead amidst the trampled grass."

Trevelyan and his comrades were lucky. More than one hunter and/or mahout (elephant handler) had been mauled or killed during such an encounter. There is at least one verified story of a tiger actually bringing down an elephant. It is no wonder then that the hunter wanted every possible safeguard he could pack into his kit.

While obviously the rifle would be the main arm of choice, should several hundred pounds of flashing teeth and claws come rocketing towards you, the gun's longer barrel might not

OUR EVALUATION HOWDAH PISTOL WAS MADE BY RODDA OF LONDON AND CALCUTTA, AND EXHIBITS MANY FEATURES SEEN ON DOUBLE RIFLES OF THE PERIOD, INCLUDING AN UNDERLEVER AND WOODEN FORE-END.

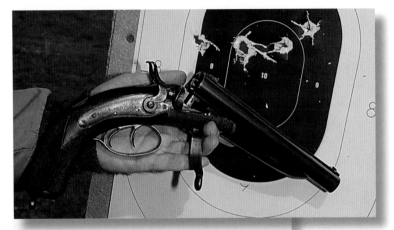

EVEN THOUGH MANY OF THE BULLETS
KEYHOLED, ACCURACY AT VARIOUS
RANGES WAS MORE THAN ACCEPTABLE
FOR THE GUN'S INTENDED PURPOSE.
THIS FOUR-SHOT 7-YARD SPREAD RAN
5 INCHES, WITH EACH BARREL GIVING
A 2-INCH GROUP.

THE BARRELS ON THE RODDA HOWDAH ARE OPENED
BY ROTATING THE GUN'S UNDERLEVER TO THE
RIGHT. THIS IS THE SAME FEATURE EMPLOYED BY
MANY BRITISH SPORTING RIFLES OF THE PERIOD.

ONE LOADS CARTRIDGES IN THE SAME MANNER HE
WOULD CHARGE A DOUBLE SHOTGUN OR RIFLE. THE
HAMMERS MUST BE PUT ON HALF COCK TO FACILI-
TATE OPENING THE ACTION.

make it easy to wield; and, too, it is possible that things happened so quickly that there simply was not time to reload. Enter the "howdah pistol."

Most of these behemoth handguns were made in the manner of rifles in that they chambered the same bone-crushing rounds and featured one or two barrels that opened by means of various types of lever.

Calibers ranged widely, but one of the more popular was the .577 Snider, the British service round from 1867 to 1873. Despite being a very powerful, effective load, it had the advantage of ready availability. While sporting rounds were sold commercially, issue ammunition could be obtained and used in a pinch. Also, some British officers carried howdah pistols into battle, as many were not pleased with the ane-mic performance of the .450 Adams round.

Needless to say, a howdah pistol was not the sort of thing one would exactly take out plink-ing. A Snider-chambered model, for example, threw a 450-grain Minié-style projectile out of a 7½-inch barrel at about 600 feet per sec-ond, for a muzzle energy of 360 foot-pounds. Compared to the hotshot of the period, the .45 Colt—which had an ME of around 420, this doesn't sound particularly impressive. But if one applies the Taylor values which, like the British ballisticians of the era, puts a premium on momentum and bullet diameter, then you have quite a different story. The Taylor value of the .45 Colt is 14, while that of the Snider is

LIKE OTHER HOWDAHS OF THE PERIOD, THE RODDA
DOUBLE CHAMBERED A LARGE-CALIBER BLACK POWDER
CARTRIDGE, IN THIS CASE THE .577 SNIDER BRITISH
SERVICE ROUND. ORIGINAL ISSUE ROUNDS WERE OF
PAPER-COVERED, COILED BRASS (LEFT.) EVALUATION
AMMO (CENTER) WAS OF DRAWN BRASS. A .41 MAGNUM
(RIGHT) IS DWARFED BY THE .577 DUO.

22—just below that of a .44 Magnum!

For our evaluation, we scratched up a mid-1870s-vintage double-barreled .577 Snider howdah sold by R.B. Rodda & Co. of London and Calcutta, a firm well known for top-grade firearms. The gun had exposed hammers, an under-lever and simple extractors. The grip was deeply curved, completely checkered around its circumference, fitted with a buttcap and lanyard ring and inset with a silver escutcheon intended for the owner's initials or crest. The sights were optimistic, consisting of a two-leaf express-style rear and rounded post front.

The gun features back-action locks, blued barrels (which may have originally been browned), a case-hardened frame and fine engraving overall. A dainty, smooth splinter fore-end completes the elegant, if somewhat formidable, package. The whole was cased, with accessories and ammunition, in a well crafted green baize-lined mahogany box. Markings on the trade label indicate that the gun had indeed seen use in British India.

To load the Rodda howdah, simply put the hammers on half cock (to allow the firing pins to back off by means of spring pressure) and then move the lever to the right to drop the barrels. Two cartridges are chambered, shotgun-style, and the barrels closed. Then aim the piece, full-cock the hammers and pull the triggers—the front for the left barrel and the right for the rear. The let-off on both triggers came in at a crisp 4½ pounds.

This all sounds as simple as pie, and it is, until the rounds go off. One then experiences wrist-wrenching recoil, the discomfort of which is abetted by a poorly-designed grip and needle-sharp checkering digging into one's palm. I loved it! Black powder .577 Snider cartridges, by the way, were supplied by that purveyor of obsolete and arcane ammunition, The Old Western Scrounger.

We shot the Rodda about 20 times at distances of 7 and 25 yards. While accuracy was certainly acceptable for "tiger groups," about half of the bullets keyholed, even at the closer targets. The .577 Snider black powder ammunition we

To remove the Rodda Howdah's barrels, simply push out the fore-end wedge, remove the fore-end and rotate the barrels down and off. Note the fine workmanship and engraving, indicative of all good-quality British sporting guns of the 19th century.

Recoil from the .577 pistol was not unsubstantial, and after shooting about 20 rounds, the author's wrist and hand were just a little bit sore. The gun's triggers were crisp and light.

used was of excellent quality and featured proper, period-style 450-grain lead hollow-based Minié bullets. G&A's resident technical expert, Bob Forker, opined that the rifling was probably just not adequate to efficiently stabilize the bullets in such short (7½-inch) barrels.

Still, at the jaw-snapping ranges these guns were supposed to be fired at, there is no doubt that if one kept one's head, and the tiger cooperated the least bit, a howdah pistol might just spell the difference between a severe mauling and an evening back in camp knocking down a few chota pegs with the "mem."

*Though lacking in power,
this Civil War-vintage cartridge revolver
was a popular self-defense arm.*

By 1836 Sam Colt had pretty well solved the repeating handgun problem, and though his early revolvers took awhile to catch on, by the time of the California Gold Rush, practically every "Argonaut" going West tried to equip himself with one of the Colonel's new five-shot pocket pistols.

There's no question these formative wheelguns gave the user a distinct advantage over an adversary armed with a single-shot pistol, for instance, and multiple balls could be sent flying in as little time as it took to thumb-cock the hammer and pull the trigger. The main problem came when one had to reload.

As the early Colts were percussion arms, it was necessary to charge each chamber in the cylinder with powder, ball and cap or use fragile paper cartridges. Even with an under-barrel loading lever this was a laborious project. In addition, the chambers were not always sealed as tightly as they could have been and were subject to absorption of moisture and the risk of a gang fire.

Some self-contained cartridges, such as the pinfire and Hunt, had been around for awhile but were generally fragile, difficult to come by and

RIGHT FROM ITS INTRODUCTION IN 1861, THE SMITH & WESSON NO. 2 ARMY WAS A HOT SELLER WITH MILITARY, POLICE AND CIVILIANS.

not all that easy to use. Given the choice, most shooters would opt for a cap-and-ball setup.

Horace Smith and Daniel Wesson had been working in the firearms business for a number of years prior to going into partnership in 1852 to manufacture a lever-action repeating handgun. But due to the cartridge's fragility and lack of power, the guns were never particularly popular. The pair eventually sold out to the Volcanic Repeating Arms Company, which continued to produce rifles and pistols until it went broke. Eventually the firm was acquired by Oliver Winchester.

In 1856 Smith and Wesson got back together again to make a product that was to revolutionize the firearms industry: the No. 1 Revolver. The No. 1 was really the first practical cartridge revolver and employed the bored-through cylinder arrangement devised by Rollin White—which is seen on virtually all revolvers today.

Now, instead of going through the laborious percussion loading procedure, it was possible to simply push a latch, swivel the revolver's barrel skyward, remove the cylinder, drop in the rounds (seven of 'em), return the cylinder to the frame, snap the barrel back into position, cock the hammer and pull the trigger.

The gun was small and the caliber, .22 Short, not exactly a man-stopper. Still, the public evidently felt the load was not bad for what was basically a pocket pistol, and soon the company had trouble keeping up with orders.

Too, the timing couldn't have been better, for in April, 1861—four years after the No. 1 appeared—the Rebels fired on Fort Sumter and the Civil War was under way. Of course there was never any serious consideration given to adopting S&W products for military use, but soldiers by the thousands began snapping them up as secondary self-protection arms. Never mind that the No. 1's cartridge was barely powerful enough to push its 29-grain bullet through the average overcoat.

Still, there were some savvy officers and men out there who realized the extra bother of lugging one of these guns along on a march (where every ounce counted), coupled with the difficulty of getting proper ammunition in the field was just not worth the bother; especially when the round was so unfit for combat.

There was no question in the minds of Messrs Smith and Wesson that something a bit more substantial was in order. And just in time for the war the company came out with a variant of its pistol, appropriately named the No. 2

AT SEVEN YARDS, GROUPS MEASURED SOME 1½ INCHES AND SLIGHTLY TO THE LEFT OF POINT OF AIM.

Army. Though the No. 2 looked and operated a lot like its predecessor, it was half again as large, and the caliber was increased to .32 Rimfire which, with its 90-grain outside lubricated bullet backed with 13 grains of black powder, gave the gun pretty much the same punch as the highly popular .31 Colt Pocket Model that fired a 50-grain ball using a 15-grain charge.

Of course, even the .31 had never been thought of as a military round. And despite the fact that it was much less potent than the .36 and .44 service loads, it was still regarded highly enough as a defense round to be taken seriously by civilians and police. This confidence unquestionably transferred over to the .32 Rimfire, and sales of the No. 2 were brisk, with some dealers charging two times the list price.

While the standard revolver was blued with plain rosewood grips, right from the beginning S&W offered fancy options to include pearl and ivory grips, engraving, special finishes and the like. Barrels could be had in 4-, 5- or 6-inch lengths; the latter appeared to be the most popular with military men.

Before its demise in 1874, some 77,155 No. 2s were manufactured and found favor with the humble, the famous and notorious. George Armstrong Custer owned a cased, engraved pair of No. 2s that were presented to him by J.B. Sutherland in 1869. A No. 2 was taken from the body of Wild Bill Hickok after he was shot by Jack McCall in 1876. Cole Younger was reported to have owned one given to him by Confederate guerrilla William Quantrill.

As the .32 RF round was chambered in a number of other handguns and rifles, it continued to be produced well into the 20th century, though the No. 2 was made obsolete fairly early by other, more sophisticated designs. In fact, S&W helped the process along when, in 1865,

A TINY NOTCH REAR SIGHT (LEFT) IS SET ATOP THE BACK PORTION OF THE MOVING CYLINDER STOP. THE FRONT SIGHT (RIGHT) IS A GERMAN SILVER BLADE DOVETAILED IN THE BARREL RIB.

it offered a Model 1½ in .32, sized midway between the No. 1 and No. 2, which continued to be offered for almost 20 years.

While No. 2s are neat-looking little repeaters that feel good in the hand, lack of ammunition has meant that in recent times they are pretty much relegated to the den wall. A few years ago, Navy Arms offered a limited run of .32 Long, as the round came to be known, loaded with smokeless powder and manufactured in Brazil. Smart people (I wasn't one of them, as usual) stocked up. I managed to secure one box, which I've been hoarding, but recently decided it was time to bust a few rounds loose and see what the No. 2 was really made of.

My evaluation revolver is a standard blued 6-incher with rosewood grips. Condition is about 60 percent, the bore is good and with the exception of a slightly loose top hinge (a common problem with these little tip-ups), and the action is tight.

While the grip is not overgenerous, it's well formed. The hammer is easy to cock, and the pull on the spur trigger is a very snappy 2½ pounds. There is no half-cock safety.

The cylinder stop is actually a spring-loaded bar on the top of the frame, which drops down into the cylinder notch when the gun is cocked. A tiny, narrow V rear sight notch is set at the back of the cylinder stop—not a great arrangement, but adequate for any use to which a No. 2 would probably be put. The front sight is a German silver rounded blade dovetailed into the barrel rib.

I took the No. 2 and Navy Arms ammo to the range for its run-through, and targets were set out at 7 yards and 25 yards. Following the procedure outlined above, loading the gun was very easy. Recoil was virtually nil, and the overall experience quite pleasant.

I quickly determined that, given the sighting limitations (I could hardly get them on target at 25 yards), it was deemed prudent to shoot the thing at 7 yards, which I did. Results were excellent with groups coming in regularly at around 1½ inches, slightly left of point-of-aim and certainly acceptable for close-range defense

Loading

(1) THE NO. 2 IS LOADED BY FLICKING THE RELEASE LATCH AND (2) TIPPING THE BARREL UPWARD. (3) THE CYLINDER IS THEN REMOVED AND (4) CARTRIDGES INSERTED IN THE INDIVIDUAL CHAMBERS. (5) ONCE THE CYLINDER IS REPLACED AND THE BARREL SNAPPED BACK INTO POSITION, THE GUN IS READY TO FIRE.

work. There were no misfires or malfunctions, attesting to the quality of firearm and ammo.

Cases are ejected from the gun by removing the cylinder and poking them out one at a time using the ejector rod.

I really don't think I would've lugged along a No. 2 if I was a Civil War soldier, but if I was a civilian living in the crime-ridden cities of New York, Washington D.C. or San Francisco in the 1860s, this handy S&W might not have been too bad a choice to slip into my coat pocket while abroad. And, if I didn't stop the footpad, at least I could have amazed him with the cleverness of the little pistol.

Colt Model 1877

The self-cocking Lightning may have had its flaws, but a lack of mystique certainly wasn't one of them.

It was the brainchild of William Mason, a designer who also served as the superintendent of Colt's Armory. Mason built the '77 around the scaled-down lines of the 1873 Army but incorporated several design elements from Colt's pocket-size New Line revolver.

It's a mystery why, with all of the successful European double-action revolvers then in existence, Mason didn't opt for something better than his own intricate and delicate system. Throughout its production, the 1877 was plagued with frequent breakage of its intricately shaped and/or highly flexed internal springs, and an action that was often out of whack. Despite this, the '77 still enjoyed modest popularity, especially on the American frontier. In the .41 Long Colt Thunderer version, it was a favorite of none other than William Bonney, a.k.a "Billy The Kid." Army scout and manhunter Tom Horn also packed a '77 Colt, as did lady bandits Pearl Hart and Belle Starr. The infamous Texas shootist John Wesley Hardin also packed a brace of .41-caliber '77s during the last couple of years of his life.

ALTHOUGH COLT REVOLVERS ARE LEGENDARY, THE COMPANY'S MODEL 1877 DOUBLE-ACTION, ORIGINALLY MARKETED AS THE "SELF-COCKER," HAS THE DUBIOUS HONOR AMONG SHOOTERS AND COLLECTORS OF HAVING THE WORST DA SYSTEM EVER DEVISED.

Despite its mechanical weaknesses, the lightning-fast action and smooth handling qualities of the '77 Colt endeared the gun to many. With a total production of 166,849 guns spanning a period of 32 years (1877-1909), the model was produced in a broad range of variations, most notably in barrel lengths, finishes, and grips.

The '77 Colt was produced in two major chamberings: .38 Long Colt and .41 Long Colt. A handful was produced in .32 Colt, but such specimens are extremely rare today.

Interestingly, the '77 Colt is better known by either of two nicknames given it by one of Colt's major distributors of the era. When the revolver was first produced, Colt simply referred to it as its New Double-Action, Self Cocking, Central Fire, Six Shot Revolver. However, since the sixgun's DA capabilities allowed for quite rapid firing, B. Kittredge of Cincinnati, Ohio, coined the nickname of Lightning for the .38-caliber version of the '77 Colt and Thunderer for the .41 model. But Lightning stuck.

Standard-grade guns were finished in handsome Colt blue with color case-hardened frames or in nickel plating, although other finishes, engraving and other deluxe options were available at extra cost. Barrel lengths ran from 1½ to 10 inches, with the norm running at 2½ to 3½ inches sans ejector (the so-called Storekeeper's Model) and 4½ to 6 inches in length with the

Fieldstripping

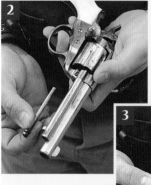

To fieldstrip an 1877 Colt, (1) bring the hammer to half-cock, open the loading gate, rotate the cylinder, check to ensure each chamber is empty. (2) With the revolver still at half-cock, extract the cylinder base pin. (3) Withdraw the cylinder from the frame.

ejector rod and housing assembly.

To be fair, when in new condition the '77 worked smoothly and efficiently. However, if the revolver was put to work very much, the inherent design weaknesses became obvious. Besides the delicate springs that were over-flexed when the gun was operated, the single-action trigger was made up of a separate sear that articulated with the trigger stud and was easily put out of order. Further, the cylinder stop used a lower arm that required a high state of tuning and was greatly strained during operation, thus making it prone to breakage. This stop was actually a small stud that protruded from the bottom left corner of the frame's rear wall. It was designed to fit into deeply cut bolt notches—slots cut at the cylinder's rear face in between each charge hole—rather than rising

up from the floor of the frame below the cylinder, as on the 1873 SAA. When the hammer was cocked, the cylinder locking stud's lower arm flexed greatly as it was forced to withdraw far enough to clear the cartridge case heads as the cylinder rotated.

Overall, the biggest weakness of the '77 Colt was that it employed a series of delicate springs that required constant tuning. Apparently, even the simplest cycling of the action could compromise its workings. But based on the longevity and production figures, gun buyers of the late 19th century were willing to overlook these weaknesses, realizing, of course, that most handguns are carried much more than they are actually fired.

I recently had the opportunity to fire several '77 Colt Lightnings in conjunction with this article. I contacted two shooting amigos, Al Frisch and Kevin Russell, both of whom have Lightnings in working order. We packed the Lightnings, some .38 Colt ammo and headed to a nearby shooting range.

Al and Kevin brought along several '77s, ranging from 2½-inch Storekeeper's to 6-inch belt models. Kevin's ammo included everything from his own homebrewed black-powder and low-pressure smokeless loads to a box of commercial Cowboy Action stuff. His black-powder fodder, incidentally, consisted of 16 grains of FFFg Goex topped with a Speer 149-grain, cast lead semi-wadcutter. His smokeless handloads were made up of three grains of Unique pushing a 150-grain semiwadcutter from Western Nevada Bullet Co. The commercial stuff was from Tennessee Cartridge Co.

There are a couple of interesting facts regarding the 1877 Colt. Although the .38 Lightning was chambered and bored for the .38 Long Colt cartridge with bores measuring .375 of an inch, at around 150,000 serial number range (1904) Colt started turning out '77s with bores measuring .356 of an inch. Cylinder specs remained constant. Because of this bore-size change, a .38 Special bullet actually fits better in the bores of post-150,000-serial-numbered guns. However, since these revolvers were produced for use with black-powder ammunition, it is

THE COLT 1877'S CYLINDER-LOCKING BOLT PROTRUDED FROM THE BREECH-FACE INSTEAD OF THE FLOOR OF THE FRAME, AS WITH THE '73 COLT SAA. THIS WAS ONE OF THE MANY WEAKNESSES OF THE LIGHTNING.

POTENTIAL PROBLEM: THE BOLT HAD TO RECESS FAR ENOUGH FROM THESE DEEP CYLINDER NOTCHES TO CLEAR THE CARTRIDGE HEAD WITH EACH SHOT.

ALTHOUGH SMALLER IN SIZE THAN THE 1873 SAA, THE 1877 DA LIGHTNING HAD THE SAME GENERAL LINES AND FUNCTION, INCLUDING LOADING AND UNLOADING.

THE CYLINDER PIN DOUBLED AS AN EXTACTOR FOR THE SHORT-BARRELED MODELS. LARGER VERSIONS FEATURED A FIXED EXTRACTOR.

our paper targeting at 7 to 15 yards, firing 5-shot groups so we could lower the hammer on an empty chamber. At 15 yards each gun was fired single action from an offhand position. Groups averaged 7½ inches. Although that's not especially impressive, the guns grouped within the torso of a silhouette target at that distance.

Moving in to 7 yards, various 5-shot patterns revealed the little six-shooter's short-range defensive potential. Firing an 1881-production 2½-inch model—stoked with black-powder loads—we were able to score a 5-shot cluster of 4⅝ inches, with the first four measuring just 2⅝ inches. A second circa-1881 gun sporting a 4½-inch tube produced a 4⅜-inch grouping with two shots touching. Kevin's 1906-vintage family heirloom with a 4½-inch tube averaged groups between 3½ and 4 inches with the largest one at 5⅝ inches and the smallest at just 1³⁄₁₆ inches.

When we switched to DA mode our accuracy was generally about the same as when the revolvers were shot as SAs—despite the extremely long trigger pull. Kevin's great-grandpa's '77—loaded with .38 Special Tennessee Cartridge Co. smokeless Cowboy Action loads—produced groups ranging from just 3 inches down to 2¹⁄₁₆ inches. One of the groups included four shots at just ¹⁵⁄₁₆ of an inch, with the first-shot flyer opening it to 2⅝ inches.

As far as handling, the Lightning loads and unloads smoothly in the traditional single-action manner, the recoil is mild and the trigger pull is even and smooth, although quite long in double-action. The sights are typical of other frontier-era six-shooters, and each of us found the bird's head grip to be comfortable despite differences in our hand sizes. We did experience a malfunction with one of the 6-inch-barreled guns and thus were unable to fire it after a single grouping was scored, but the rest of our 1877s performed flawlessly.

I have to admit that after firing this assortment of Lightnings, I have a new respect for the accuracy potential and overall ergonomics of the Colt '77, despite its delicate innards.

not a good idea to use standard-power smokeless ammo in any of these old guns. In the later-production models, certain low-pressure .38 Special Cowboy Action loads—generating around 750 fps—may be used but only after the gun has been checked out by a gunsmith.

Since the '77 was produced as a medium-powered defensive handgun, we decided to do

CLASSIC TEST

Remington's .41 Rimfire Derringer has become
as much of a symbol of the Old West
as the Colt Peacemaker.

Despite its anemic bite, the .41 Rimfire Remington Over/Under Derringer was in production for nearly 70 years. It was a popular hideout gun for "ladies of the night," gamblers, gunfighters and lawmen that became as much of a symbol of the Old West as the venerable Colt Peacemaker.

The overwhelming success of the Remington Derringer in .41 Rimfire sharply contrasts with its completely underwhelming power. The latter never mattered much, though. It is arguable that the fear of being shot with anything in the 19th century was a more powerful fight-stopper than the deed itself. Often, any torso wound was an eventual fatality. Even a picayune wound in an era that lacked competent first aid could be disastrous if allowed to become infected. Because of this general fear, coupled with the psychological effect of the big twin .41 caliber barrels sported by the Remington, more fights were probably stopped by the presence of the derringer than by its actual discharge.

Then, as now, small pistols found great favor with the public, and the Remington two-shot was a "best-of-class" firearm. Other makes of similar caliber, such as the Colt No. 1 or the earlier Henry Deringer Derringers and their copies, were single-shot varieties and were not much smaller in size. The Remington outlasted them all and enjoyed a long production run that lasted from 1866 to 1935, almost seven decades. It was the last Remington-manufactured handgun until the XP-100 some 40 years later. One of America's most prolific designers, William Eliot, came up with the O/U Derringer in 1865. His is a sturdy design that involves a cam which moves the firing pin up or down when the hammer is cocked, so that it always selects the next barrel for action. A simple lever on the side of the frame moves past a ball-detent 180 degrees to unlatch the barrels and permit them to swing up for loading and unloading. The first models, made until 1869, had no extractor. After that, the guns came

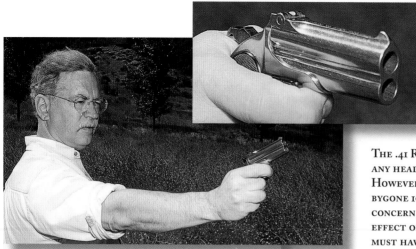

THE .41 RF ROUND HAS NEVER TURNED
ANY HEADS AS A FIGHT-STOPPER.
HOWEVER, ANY GUNSHOT WOUNDS IN THE
BYGONE 19TH CENTURY WERE OF GREAT
CONCERN, AND THE PSYCHOLOGICAL
EFFECT OF THE TWO LARGE "BLACK EYES"
MUST HAVE BEEN INTIMIDATING.

RECOIL OF THE LIGHT LITTLE DERRINGER WAS
BRISK DESPITE ITS ANEMIC ROUND, CAUSING SOME
CONCERN ABOUT THE POWER OF THE NAVY ARMS
AMMO. GARRY JAMES, WHO HAS FIRED ORIGINAL
BLACK-POWDER ROUNDS, STATES THAT THE
ORIGINAL .41 RF GENERATES FAR LESS RECOIL IN
COMPARISON. THE REMINGTON SUFFERED NO
UNTOWARD EFFECTS, HOWEVER.

A CAM INSIDE THE
DERRINGER AUTOMATI-
CALLY MOVES THE FIR-
ING PIN UP OR DOWN
WHEN THE HAMMER IS
COCKED AND AUTO-
MATICALLY SELECTS
THE UNFIRED BARREL.
IT IS A SIMPLE AND
RUGGED DESIGN THAT
IS STILL IN USE.

SIGHTS ON THE
REMINGTON ARE A SIM-
PLE U-NOTCH REAR
AND BLADE FRONT.
CONSIDERING THE
RANGE AT WHICH THIS
LITTLE GUN IS INTEND-
ED TO BE USED, THEY
ARE PERFECTLY ADE-
QUATE AND, PERHAPS
MORE IMPORTANT,
SNAG-FREE.

to allow the placement of the Derringer up the
sleeve of a coat. Some of these holsters spring-
loaded the derringer and would launch the little
gun into the shooting hand. The hammer's
half-cock notch is the only safety present, and
it is important to half-cock the hammer prior
to loading lest closing the loaded barrels briskly
discharge the gun.

The Derringer went through little mechanical
change throughout its production life. Collectors
categorize six different models based mostly
on address variations rather than mechanical
changes, except for the addition of extractors and
minor changes in the rifling.

Our test Derringer was a fifth model made
between 1888 and 1910. It is in excellent condition, having about 98 percent of its nickel plate,
with its nitre blued small parts beginning to
turn plum. As expected of a Remington product
from any era, the derringer was well-fitted with
excellent polish to the parts and no looseness.
The barrels exhibited somewhat lackadaisical
care from former owners, but we felt the small
amount of pitting present wouldn't affect accuracy, nor did we anticipate minute of angle
performance either. Indeed, we shot our target
at 7 yards, feeling that would be the maximum
range at which such a pistol would be deployed.
Although we had no original black-powder
ammunition—and might think twice before
using any of these increasingly rare specimens—
we had a goodly number of late Navy Arms .41
Rimfire rounds for the test.

Speed-loading and rapid reloading is not

with a simple thumb-operated ejector that
started the empties from the chambers simul-
taneously. The Remington is truly a palm-sized
gun and fits comfortably in a vest or trouser
pocket, although clever holsters were invented

this pistol's forte. It is a "last-ditch" weapon that serves as an effective bludgeon when grasped by the barrels—and some might say it is more effective that way. Still, 7-yard accuracy with the simple U-notch and blade front sights was quite good. Both shots were centered windage-wise, with the one shot in the 9-ring and the other about 2½ inches higher in the 7-ring—plenty accurate for the derringer's intended mission. Functioning was flawless and the Navy Arms shells dropped from the chambers easily. Being that they were of copper-case construction, the extractor was sometimes necessary to start them moving.

The little .41 Short Rimfire cartridge was developed in 1863 for the National Arms Co. single-shot Derringer. It launched its 130-grain, .41 caliber, outside-lubricated, heel-based bullet at 425 feet per second, which generated 52 foot-pounds of muzzle energy. Many companies made guns for this little round, either Derringers or revolvers of the "bulldog" size. Ammunition was produced until World War II.

Our Navy Arms test ammo was from the last lot made in Brazil during the late 1980s, and Navy Arms has no plans to make any more. Still, the diligent gunshow hunter can turn a box or two up now and then if he's persistent, although the tariff gets higher with the passing years. However, the anemic performance of the cartridge argues against its use for anything but the odd Cowboy Action sidematch, while some argue that today's smokeless powder loads should not be used in these old black-powder derringers at all. The factories in the United States put together black-powder loads for these little guns through all but the last years of its production.

The Remington Derringer is one of the Old West's more enduring icons, one that stands alongside the Colt Peacemaker and Winchester '73. It remained in production for as many years as the first-generation Colt and for more years than the Winchester. It did its job well, and today it is rewarded with many imitations, perhaps the sincerest form of flattery.

Loading

To load the Remington Derringer: (1) Place the hammer in its half-cock position and turn the locking-lever 180 degrees counterclockwise to unlatch the barrels. (2) Tip the barrels up to expose the chambers and (3) insert the cartridges. (4) Close the barrels and turn the lever back to its detent to lock. The derringer unloads the same way as it loads. A thumb-activated extractor may be employed to start the cases from the chambers.

*This handy Royal Irish Constabulary variant
is the ultimate Victorian bulldog.*

When one thinks of British handguns the name that immediately comes to mind is "Webley." Never mind that Robert Adams first put English revolvers on par with some of the best the Americans had to offer, or that William Tranter was a much better-known maker than Philip Webley in the early years. No, it's Webley that sticks in the public's mind—with good reason. By the 1880s the firm had come out with one of the fastest, most perfect loading/ejection mechanisms ever devised: the top-break, stirrup-latch system.

To those steeped in British colonial exploits during the latter part of the 19th century it's difficult to imagine any of the maker's other products that can match the large-frame .455s. But there was one, and without it there is a very good chance that the name Webley wouldn't be the recognizable trademark it now is.

In the percussion era, if one went to a gun-shop in London or Birmingham, it's likely he would be shown an Adams, Tranter, Daw or the like. To be sure, Webley had certainly come up with some fine revolvers by the 1850s, but they were definitely not in the forefront of

NOTHING EVOKES VICTORIAN LONDON LIKE THE WEBLEY METROPOLITAN POLICE REVOLVER. IT'S AS MUCH A PART OF THE SCENE AS SHERLOCK HOLMES' LONG-STEM BRIAR PIPE OR A BOBBY'S WHISTLE.

popularity. Adams had secured the first major government contract with his Beaumont DA, and this basic gun—in caplock and cartridge versions—would remain preeminent with the military for a number of years.

But Webley products continued to improve and evolve, and in 1867 the company introduced a solid-frame repeater that was to become a boon to its business. The Royal Irish Constabulary (RIC) revolver took its name from the force that first adopted it in 1868. The gun was introduced in .442 centerfire, which employed a 200-grain bullet backed with 15 grains of black powder. It featured an extremely simple action and ejection system, involving a swiveling rod housed within the cylinder pin.

Cartridges were loaded into the cylinder through a downward pivoting gate. When they had been expended, the gun was put on half-cock, the gate opened, and the ejector rod twisted to unlatch it, pulled forward and turned to the right. Now all one had to do was poke out the empties one at a time. The arrangement was fast, simple and efficient, and in fairly short order RICs appeared in a large number of calibers, including .430, .450, .455, .476, .45 Colt and .44-40.

The beauty of the design was that it could be adapted to a wide variety of configurations. There were "military" models and other vari-

THE EVALUATION M.P. SHOT LOW AND TO THE RIGHT. THIS RESTED GROUP, USING FIOCCHI 226-GRAIN SMOKELESS LOADS, MEASURES 1⅝ INCHES.

THE .450 SERVICE ROUND (LEFT) EMPLOYS A 225-GRAIN BULLET BACKED BY 13 GRAINS OF BLACK POWDER. THE .450 ROUND DEVELOPS 211 FT-LBS OF MUZZLE ENERGY WHILE THE COLT .45, (RIGHT), HAS A MUZZLE ENERGY OF 420 FT-LBS.

THE CYLINDER IS REMOVED BY SETTING THE GUN ON HALF-COCK, OPENING THE LOADING GATE, PULLING OUT THE EJECTOR ROD AND SLIDING OUT THE CYLINDER PIN.

THE METROPOLITAN POLICE HOLDS WELL AND HAS PLEASANT SINGLE- AND DOUBLE-ACTION TRIGGER PULLS. RECOIL WITH THE FIOCCHI AMMO WAS A TAD ON THE STOUT SIDE.

ants of differing barrel lengths and grip shapes, including the stubby Bulldogs of popular fancy. (As an aside, the terms "bulldog" and associated "barker" and "snapper" derived from 18th century slang for mid-sized flintlock pistols).

The RIC was one of the most-copied revolvers of its era, and look-alikes were produced in Belgium, Spain and the United States.

The first version of the RIC can immediately be recognized by its forward cylinder locking notches. This was deemed not totally satisfactory by the makers, so the more common rear locking design was introduced in 1872 and remained standard throughout the gun's production. Many different barrels were offered and some of the shorter ones dispensed with the ejection system, it probably being surmised that, as these guns were to be carried for personal protection, it was unlikely the user would need to resort to more than five or six shots. If the footpads hadn't been dissuaded by then, there was a very good chance that the row would have attracted one of London's many Peelers (an early nickname for police constables), who would then deal with the situation.

In 1880 one of the more popular RIC versions, the Metropolitan & County Police Model, made its debut. It was originally introduced in .450 caliber (225-grain bullet, 23 grains of black powder) but later on, .455s (265-grain bullet, 18 grains of black powder) were also made available. It had a solid frame and swiveling ramrod setup. Though the frame and grip remained the same size as those on a standard model, the barrel was reduced to 2½ inches. It was double-action, but could also be thumb-cocked for more deliberate shooting. Grips were usually checkered walnut, capped with a baseplate and lanyard ring. Cylinders were smooth or fluted, depending when the gun was made. Sights were fixed and involved a simple blade front and V-notch rear set at the back of a groove in the topstrap.

Markings included the standard Webley address on the frame and a roll-engraved representation of a pair of manacled hands surrounded by the words "WEBLEY'S M.P."

Despite its size and heft (some 10 ounces more than a pound), the Metropolitan immediately found favor with law enforcement and civilians alike. It was sturdy, reliable, reasonably powerful and able to be concealed readily in the pocket of an ulster or greatcoat.

Metropolitan Police Revolvers received worldwide distribution and it's not unusual to see examples stamped "NZ" (New Zealand), "NSW" (New South Wales) or with some other Colonial markings. While standard police versions were blued, some constabulary guns were nickel-plated. A Webley M.P. in my collection has a deeply stamped "POLICE" and "1222" (presumably a rack or issue number.)

Though the .450 caliber is not a round normally encountered, fortunately it's loaded in smokeless powder by Fiocchi. The cartridges are a tad stouter in recoil than their black-powder predecessors and employ 226-grain RN lead bullets. Proper case and rim dimensions have been maintained.

It might be noted that one of the problems reloaders have when trying to fabricate British revolver rounds from American brass is the English cartridges' thin rims. This means many cases, such as .45 Colt, have to have a bit of rear-end lathe work done. But in my case I was supplied with a box of Fiocchi .450s and packed the M.P. off to the range for a run-through.

Optimistically I set up the first targets at 25 yards, and let fly (deliberately, of course) from a rest. Not one of the bullets hit the board, and after two more attempts, I brought the targets into a range of 7 yards. Rested, single-action groups measured in the 1⅝-inch range, though the gun shot about three inches low and 3½ inches to the right. As the sights are fixed, I employed Kentucky windage with some joy when shooting the gun offhand, DA. These spreads hit closer to the center of the bull and measured some 2½ inches.

The gun feels very good in the hand, and the SA trigger came in at a crisp 3½ pounds, while the double-action pull was a smooth 10 pounds. Empties were easily expelled with the

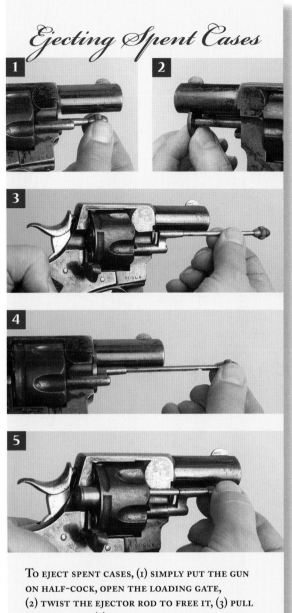

Ejecting Spent Cases

TO EJECT SPENT CASES, (1) SIMPLY PUT THE GUN ON HALF-COCK, OPEN THE LOADING GATE, (2) TWIST THE EJECTOR ROD TO FREE IT, (3) PULL OUT THE ROD, (4) SWIVEL IT TO THE RIGHT AND (5) POKE OUT THE SHELL.

clever rotating ejector rod, though it did not extend all the way to the rear of the chamber and a sharp thrust was necessary to pop the cases clear of the holes.

If you're of the romantic turn of mind the Webley Metropolitan Police Revolver, or any RIC for that matter, is a must-have. Be forewarned, though, that after getting one it's not at all unusual to acquire a taste for bully beef, Camp Coffee, music hall ditties and Bovril.

Colt .25 Pocket Hammerless

Great design, coupled with high quality,

made this one of the top hideout guns

of the 1920s and '30s.

Over the years, I've tested just about every new (and old) pocket pistol that's come down the pike...including some pretty exotic European examples, and I still think the one to beat was John Browning's .25 ACP Hammerless Colt effort of 1908.

It was among the smallest of Browning's pistol designs...sort of an abbreviated version of his classic Model 1903 .32 Pocket Model.

Actually, the Colt "Vest Pocket" as it has come to be called, had its antecedents in Belgium, where it was initially introduced in 1906 and manufactured by Fabrique Nationale. It became an instant hit, and as the "Model 1906 Baby Browning" (the latter name was eventually applied to a 1920 incarnation of the gun that dispensed with the grip safety, among

DURING THE '20S AND '30S, THE COLT POCKET HAMMERLESS WAS A POPULAR HIDEOUT GUN WITH GANGSTERS AND LAW ENFORCEMENT ALIKE. IT HAD A 33-YEAR LIFESPAN. GUN AND ACCESSORIES FROM AUTHOR'S COLLECTION.

other things) was produced in great numbers for some 40 years.

In 1908 Colt decided that this would be a good item to make for sale in the U.S., and it produced the gun under license. Like the European piece, it had a grip safety, safety catch on the rear, left side of the frame, 2-inch barrel, and six-round magazine. As well, beginning at serial number 141,000, the gun had a magazine safety, whereby when the mag was removed from the gun a disconnector broke all contact between the trigger and the sear.

Functioning of the gun was assiduously described in the original instructions thusly: "The action of this pistol is automatic, except that the trigger must be pulled to fire each shot (continued discharge will not result from one pull of the trigger), the cartridges being supplied from a detachable magazine inserted in the handle of the first cartridge into the chamber. On pulling the trigger the cartridge is fired, the empty shell ejected and a new cartridge loaded into the chamber, all these

THE RECOIL SPRING IS NOT
SO STOUT AS TO PREVENT
CHAMBERING A ROUND EAS-
ILY. THE GUN IS SMALL, BUT
CAN BE MANIPULATED BY
ANYONE WITH AVERAGE-
SIZED HANDS.

MEASURING BUT 4½ INCHES OVERALL,
THE "VEST POCKET" WAS EASY TO CON-
CEAL, AND WITH ITS GRIP SAFETY, SAFETY
CATCH AND (ABOVE SERIAL NUMBER
141,000) MAGAZINE SAFETY, THOUGHT TO
BE VIRTUALLY FOOLPROOF. THE AUTHOR
STILL RECOMMENDS THAT SUCH GUNS
NOT BE CARRIED CHAMBERED, COCKED
AND LOCKED.

operations taking place automatically without
any manipulation of the arm. This automatic
operation is effected by recoil of the moving
parts and as a consequence, the recoil being
thus utilized, it is absorbed so that it has no
disturbing effect. The first shot can be discharged more quickly than from any other
arm, as this pistol can be carried with perfect
safety while the hammer is at full cock."

The finish of the standard pistol was blue
with a case-hardened trigger and grip safety.
Grips were initially of checkered hard rubber
embellished with the Colt name
and rampant colt motif and later
of checkered walnut with inset
Colt escutcheons.

Overall the diminutive pistol
measured only 4½ inches and
hefted a comfortable 13 ounces…
just about the right size to slip in a
gent's vest pocket, hence the gun's
"vest pocket" nickname. Of course,
there were fancy, embellished versions with nickel-plating, engraving, pearl or ivory grips, inlay,

THE POCKET
HAMMERLESS' SAFETY/
SLIDE STOP IS SITED ON
THE REAR, LEFT OF THE
FRAME. BECAUSE OF THE
GUN'S SIZE, IT TAKES A BIT
OF FIDDLING TO GET IT
INTO THE PROPER POSI-
TION TO EMPLOY IT.

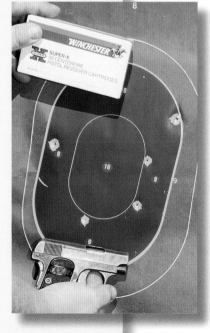

OUR TEST GUN TURNED IN AMAZING
25-YARD GROUPS FOR A .25 AUTO WITH
2-INCH BARREL. ALL SPREADS RAN
ABOUT 5 INCHES TO POINT OF AIM.
AMMO USED WAS WINCHESTER
45-GRAIN EXPANDING POINT.

etc. In fact it became a popular carry gun with Prohibition-era gangsters, who were willing to trade on the anemic .25 ACP ballistics for the element of surprise. As well as civilian use, the little Vest Pocket was also drafted into the service during World War II where, in parkerized guise, they were issued in limited numbers to the OSS and other specialized units.

The pistol fieldstrips easily...pretty much in the same manner as its bigger brother. First remove the magazine and ensure the gun is unloaded, then withdraw the slide about 3/8 inch, grasp the barrel by the serrations on the muzzle and turn it clockwise about one-quarter turn until the lugs at the rear of the barrel disengage from the slots in the frame. The slide may now be withdrawn forward off the frame and the recoil spring/rod and barrel removed from the front of the slide and the firing pin, mainspring and mainspring guide from the rear.

Our evaluation Pocket Model Hammerless was a good-condition (about 80 percent) example made in 1914. It was a standard blued model with hard-rubber grips, no magazine safety and the original magazine. The trigger was measured at a crisp 5 pounds. We took the sprout to the Petersen Ranch in Lake Los Angeles, California, along with a good supply of Winchester 45-grain Expanding Point .25s. First groups were essayed offhand at a "combat" range of 7 yards, where the little spud, as expected, dropped all six of its rounds in the black. This exercise was repeated to monotony, so for the heck of it, we bench-rested it and took a few shots at 25 yards. Lo and behold, groups stayed regularly within 5 inches at point of aim...all the more remarkable when one realizes that the teeny front blade and skimpy rear-notch sights are really not adequate for any kind of target work. In some 50 rounds, we had nary a failure to feed or eject. Based upon the above performance, if the caliber wasn't so anemic, I would seriously consider this as a handy carry gun. As it is, the Vest Pocket can at least be respected as a well crafted, exquisitely designed classic that it is.

Fieldstripping

To fieldstrip the Colt Pocket Hammerless, (1) remove the magazine and ensure the gun is unloaded. (2) Next, withdraw the slide about 3/8 inch and rotate the barrel one-quarter turn clockwise. (3) Move the slide forward off the frame. (4) Remove the recoil spring and guide. (5) Remove the barrel.

CLASSIC TEST

*This post-war .22 self-loader
remains one of the top plinkers of all time.*

One of my earliest firearms-related memories involves an evening in 1950 when my father brought home a Hi-Standard Model GB .22 that he had just talked some guy at the movie studio out of. Loaded with Remington .22 LR hollowpoints, it became our "house gun" and was the first pistol I ever fired.

To be fair, if my initiation into the world of handgunnery had involved a pot-metal Rohm .22, there is every good chance that it would have not been chosen for evaluation. But—nostalgia aside—High Standard made some of the finest .22 auto pistols ever, and that's really what qualifies my GB as worthy of a look-see.

The High Standard Company began life in 1926 as Connecticut tool makers producing drills for boring firearms barrels. This endeavor lasted about six years, when High Standard purchased the equipment of the Hartford Arms Co. in a bankruptcy sale, after which it began turning out the old Hartford-style pistols under its own name. Not satisfied with making versions of its defunct predecessor's autos, High Standard began improving its line, and pretty soon was garnering praise for its fine wares.

Civilian sales were suspended in 1942, when High Standard began selling training pistols to the U.S. military—most notably the Hi-Standard Model B (Author's Note: To avoid semantic confusion, "High" refers to the actual company. "Hi" is used to designate each model.) This gun, in its G.I. guise, was parkerized and "Property of U.S." was stamped on the frame, along with an Ordnance Department insignia. Other early autos in the lineup included the Model A, which was similar to the B but with a fixed rear sight; the Model D, which was the same as the Model A but with a heavy barrel; and a Model C in .22 Short. Later, these guns were brought out in external hammer versions, and then given an "H" prefix. One gun, the H-D Military, was also offered as a trainer and continued in production into the 1950s, when it was sold commercially as the HD-M.

In 1947 a "G" series was introduced. Their most interesting feature was the fact that barrels could be interchanged by simply pushing forward on a lever on the front of the triggerguard. The first G was chambered in .380 auto but was not popular because it was too large for a hideout pistol and just not accurate enough for target work.

THE HI-STANDARD GB AUTO WAS A WELL-MADE, WELL-ENGINEERED PISTOL THAT EXHIBITS THE USUAL QUALITY OF GUNS PRODUCED IN THE 1940S AND '50S. THE LINES AND SUPERB FINISH OF THE GB PEG IT AS A PRODUCT OF PRE- AND POST-WAR AMERICA. IT'S OF ALL-STEEL CONSTRUCTION, POSSESSES A PLEASING HEFT AND IS QUITE WELL-BALANCED.

BASICALLY A PLINKER, THE GB HAS FAIRLY SIMPLE SIGHTS, CONSISTING OF A FIXED SQUARE BLADE FRONT (TOP) AND SQUARE NOTCH REAR (BOTTOM) THAT CAN BE DRIFT ADJUSTED FOR WINDAGE.

LIKE OTHER HI-STANDARDS OF THE PERIOD, THE GB HAS A GENEROUS, WELL-SITUATED SAFETY CATCH LOCATED ON THE REAR LEFT SIDE OF THE FRAME.

LOADING THE HI-STANDARD'S MAGAZINE IS SIMILAR TO LOADING THE LUGER'S IN THAT A SIDE-MOUNTED BUTTON ALLOWS THE FOLLOWER TO BE LOWERED MANUALLY FOR EASY CARTRIDGE INSERTION.

ALTHOUGH THE CARBON BUILD-UP IS QUITE EVIDENT, THE GB STILL FUNCTIONED FLAWLESSLY FOR 150 ROUNDS.

On the other hand, Gs in .22 LR became pretty hot items. First offered in 1949, the family included the GB, which had a drift-adjustable rear sight; a heavy-barrel GD; a deluxe GE with a heavy barrel and "Davis" adjustable sights; and a G-O, which was similar to the GE but chambered for .22 Short and employed an aluminum slide.

Finish was blue and grips were brown checkered plastic with an encircled "HS" monogram in the center (with the exception of the GE and G-O, which had hand-checkered walnut grips with thumb rests.) Magazines held 10 rounds and were secured by a heel-mounted knurled catch. Barrels were offered in 4½- or 6¾-inch lengths.

In 1950 the lever was replaced with a push button takedown catch, and the guns rechristened "Olympic" (.22 Short) and "Supermatic"—though original-style Gs continued to be made until 1951. While the Supermatics—and their ilk—were offered in many variations throughout the years, a thorough discussion of them, and subsequent Hi-Standards, is out of the scope (and space availability) of this particular article. Let it suffice that High Standard made thousands of excellent .22 auto pistols (and revolvers, derringers, rifles and shotguns) until the original firm ceased production in 1984.

Currently the new High Standard manufacturing Company in Houston, Texas, is offering Supermatics, Olympics and the like.

Thanks to my dad's meticulous care, the evaluation GB is still in nice shape—in fact, it has about 99 percent of its original blue, the grips are in pretty good nick and the magazine in tip-top condition. Overall quality of the piece is hard to fault. It's machined entirely out of steel and has a pleasing heft, accentuated by excellent balance. While most of the gun is finished in a high gloss blue, attractive matte accents on the top of the slide, the front and sides of the triggerguard and around the gripstrap give the gun a pretty classy appearance. Workmanship is superb—what one has come to expect from American firearms made in the 1940s and '50s.

The round barrel measures 6¾ inches in length.

The square blade front sight is fixed, but the rear notch is drift adjustable. There are a pair of small index marks on the sight base and slide to show proper midpoint alignment.

While the grip is not very large—it might give a bit of trouble to someone with large hands—it fits me just fine. Despite the panels being little more than slightly rounded checkered slabs, the grips provide a nice hold.

The safety catch is a generous latch sited on the left rear of the slide, where it can easily be flicked off with the thumb—up for "safe," down for "fire." Even the heel magazine catch is not all that awkward to manipulate because a generous forward projecting lip on the floorplate provides good purchase for pulling the magazine from its well. Perhaps the only fault I can find with the setup is in the magazine itself. It has one of those Luger-style buttons to assist in loading. As the tension is increased, it can get a bit tricky to hold while inserting cartridges.

GB triggers are smooth and fairly narrow; that's probably why my father opted to screw on a ribbed trigger shoe, an addition that I have left on the pistol for old time's sake. The pull, by the way, came in at 3¾ pounds after a minuscule bit of takeup.

Stripping the GB is just about as simple as it can get. First remove the magazine and ensure that the gun is unloaded. Then lift up on the takedown latch and slide the barrel off the frame, followed by the slide. When you do get inside, you'll see that there is a pretty simple action, but one that's certainly built like the proverbial masonry commode.

My shooting test was essayed at the Angeles Range in San Fernando, California. Chosen .22 Long Rifle ammo was CCI Standard Velocity, Quik-Shok Hyper-Velocity and Federal Target. The gun functioned well with all three, and in 150 rounds there were no malfunctions. It was comfortable and fun to shoot, with the best 25-yard rested groups coming in at 1¼ inches at point of aim—about all that one can expect from a plinking-grade auto pistol. Best spreads

were fired with the Federal ammunition, though the others performed just fine, as well. Offhand I was consistently able to hit 25- and 50-yard metal targets with little difficulty.

In terms of quality, I'll stand my old GB up against any Colt Woodsman or Smith & Wesson 41 of the period. It's a gun that certainly lives up to its name—Hi-Standard.

Fieldstripping

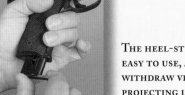

THE HEEL-STYLE MAGAZINE CATCH IS EASY TO USE, AND THE MAG EASY TO WITHDRAW VIA A GENEROUS FORWARD PROJECTING LIP ON ITS FLOORPLATE.

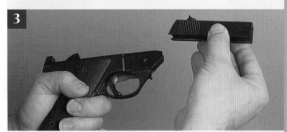

FIELDSTRIPPING THE GB IS EASY. FIRST REMOVE THE MAGAZINE AND ENSURE THAT THE GUN IS UNLOADED. (1) NOW PUSH FORWARD ON THE TAKEDOWN LATCH (2) AND TAKE OFF THE BARREL AND (3) THE SLIDE. REASSEMBLE IN REVERSE ORDER.

*This big-framed brute
is a jewel from the dawn of the magnum era.*

The world of handguns changed forever on April 8, 1935, when the .357 Magnum cartridge was officially announced. The maker of the first revolver strong enough to take this powerful new cartridge was Smith & Wesson, but over nearly seven decades scores of manufacturers have added the .357 to their list of chamberings. In the late 1930s Smith & Wesson was in fierce competition with Colt, so it's not surprising that within months of S&W's announcement, Colt was producing .357s. This story is about the first Colt revolver chambered for the new and potent round—the famed New Service .357.

Actually, I've weaseled a bit on claiming that the New Service was Colt's first .357 Magnum. Although I have consulted several respected Colt references, I'm unable to pin down the date the first New Service .357s left the plant. The same references generally agree that Colt Single-Action Army .357 revolvers were made in 1935. Colt's 1936 price lists announce both SAAs and New Services in .357, so it is possible that the new caliber was a late-1935 introduction in both models. The more important point is simply that Colt quickly saw the potential of the new cartridge and hastened to offer its biggest, strongest revolvers for it.

At any rate, the New Service .357 is surely one of the rarest Colt revolvers in this caliber. (The Peacemaker .357 returned to production after WWII, but the New Service .357 died around 1943.)

From 1898 until the beginning of WWII, more than 356,000 New Service revolvers were made. It's an aptly named model. In the late 19th century, all gunmakers were busily updating their firearms to take advantage of smokeless powder. The New Service was assuredly new and also a service revolver in the sense of a gun intended to be holster-carried by police

THE NEW SERVICE IS A BIG-FRAME DOUBLE-ACTION THAT REMAINED IN THE COLT CATALOG FOR MORE THAN 40 YEARS—BUT THE .357 VERSION WAS ONLY MADE FOR SEVEN YEARS. IN 1941 IT LISTED FOR $43.50.

SMALL BORE SIZE, BIGGER FRAME: THE NEW
SERVICE .357 (TOP) IS CONSIDERABLY MORE GUN
THAN THE .38 OFFICIAL POLICE (BOTTOM).

and military personnel. "Service" also implies the size and strength to take the most powerful, large-caliber ammunition available then. Over the 40-plus years of the New Service production run, it was chambered in .45 Colt, .44-40, .44 Special, .38-40 and a number of the British bigbores as well. There are indications that the steel for the cylinder may have been updated for the .357, and, of course, there's ample room for six chambers.

The New Service is a big gun, with a butt section that is larger and sits higher than its contemporary and main competition, the S&W .44 Hand Ejector N-frame. It has a rugged, uncomplicated look to it, with a plain round barrel screwed into its big frame. There is no shroud—or other protection—for the ejector rod. As is typical of all Colt double-action revolvers, the thumb latch is on the left side of the frame and pulls to the rear to unlatch the cylinder.

All .357 Magnum New Services are of the style Colt collectors describe as Late Models—the rounded cylinder latch very much resembles that of the familiar Colt Python. My particular

New Service is entirely typical of the breed. When it came into my possession, it was equipped with a pair of imitation stag grips made of plastic. They looked like hell on a nice old gun, so I replaced them with a pair of correct brown plastic grips with Colt medallions.

My gun was made in 1939 and has a rather uncommon—but practical—5-inch barrel. It weighs approximately 42 ounces and runs 10½ inches in overall length. A 1941 Colt price sheet advises that the gun was available with a lanyard ring at no extra cost and should sell for the princely sum of $43.50. The same price sheet tells us that for a mere $9.25 more, a shooter could have a much-upgraded New Service variant called the Shooting Master in the same caliber. That extra money got you a hand-tuned action, adjustable sights and carefully checkered frontstrap and backstrap. In the late 1930s the nation was beginning to pull out of the Great Depression, but $43.50 was still a lot of money.

I came by my gun a couple of years ago by way of a trade with gunsmith Terry Tussey. It shows relatively light wear, with about 90 percent of the original blueing remaining, except on the backstrap. There are no signs of abuse and little evidence of extensive firing. The gun appears to have been carried some and fired moderately. The double-action trigger pull weight is about 12 pounds; the single-action pull is just under four, with a very clean break.

Many shooters have difficulty reaching the trigger of a New Service with enough space to effectively work the gun in double-action mode. This is a function of the grip shape and dimensions. I rather like the Colt grip shape because it positions the hand high on the backstrap, affording good leverage against the trigger when shooting double-action. If I were going to fire the gun extensively, I would probably dig up one of the old Pachmayr grip adapt-

LIKE MOST COLT REVOLV-
ERS OF THE EARLY 20TH
CENTURY, THE EJECTOR
ROD IS UNPROTECTED IN
ITS POSITION UNDER THE
BARREL.

THE BUTT SECTION
ON A NEW SERVICE IS
QUITE LARGE AND
SETS THE HAND
ABOVE AND BEHIND
THE TRIGGER.

PULL BACK ON THE
CYLINDER LATCH,
AND SWING THE SIX-
ROUND CYLINDER OUT
TO THE LEFT.

THE ROUNDED, CHECKERED CYLINDER LATCH MARKS
THIS SPECIMEN AS A LATE MODEL.

ers to fill the space behind the triggerguard and protect the knuckle of my middle finger from a beating. Better yet, I might have Herrett's carve out a pair of Roper-style stocks for the gun. But even as-is, recoil with stout loads is not unbearable. Forty-two ounces of good Yankee steel soaks up a lot of bump and snort.

I believe this early .357 Colt may have the same 1:14 rifling pattern as the later Python because my results using the Ransom Rest turned out to be impressive indeed.

I took the big Colt to the range with an array of current-production .357 ammunition that included PMC 150-grain JHPs, Black Hills 158-grain JHPs, Winchester Super-X JHPs, Pro-Load 180-grain FPJs, Remington 180-grain SJHPs and Federal 180-grain Hi-Shok JHPs. After some informal shooting to get a feel for the old brute, I bolted it into my Ransom Rest and shot for groups. It performed

very nicely, shooting groups as small as 1.72 inches (with the Federal 180s). The average group size was just a little over two inches. I believe that a more in-depth shoot might produce even better accuracy, but I didn't trade another guy out of this old classic because I wanted to compete with it.

In terms of velocity, the fastest load that I clocked (through an Oehler Model 35 chronograph) turned out to be Winchester's 158-grain load, which registered 1,305 fps through the Colt's 5-inch barrel.

The Colt New Service represents a significant chunk of handgunning history, an old-time design made right at the dawn of the magnum era. New Service revolvers armed such diverse organizations as the border patrol, Canadian Mounties, New York State Troopers and WWI doughboys.

It's a classic that shoots.

Classic Shotguns

Classic Shotguns
Winchester Model 1877

In terms of 10-gauge intimidation,
this lever-action shotgun served as the long arm
of the law in the Old West.

The old axiom "God created man but it was Sam Colt who made them equal" might well have been true, but in 1887 John Browning and the Winchester Repeating Arms Company made both lawmen and bad men just a little more equal with the introduction of a six-shot lever-action shotgun chambered in either 12- or 10- gauge.

A pistolero pressed into a fight with the law might think twice when the barrel of a Winchester Model 1887 10-gauge was leveled at him. But in a sticky situation, every town sheriff and deputy marshal from the Texas panhandle to California knew they were going to need more than two shots from a scatter-gun at one time or another.

Winchester had pioneered the lever-action design with the Henry, and it seemed only natural, then, that when Winchester decided to build a repeating shotgun, it would be a lever-action design.

ORIGINALLY PRICED AT AROUND $25, THE MODEL 1887 LEVER-ACTION SHOTGUN WAS ONE OF THE LANDMARK WINCHESTER DESIGNS BY JOHN M. BROWNING.

The Winchester Model 1887 was designed by John M. Browning and Matthew S. Browning of Ogden City, Utah, and patented by the Winchester Repeating Arms Co. on February 16 and July 20, 1886. Initially available only in 12 gauge, a 10 gauge was offered after serial number 22148.

As noted by George Madis in *The Winchester Book*, the action on the 1887 was entirely different from the Winchester rifles, and was a variation of the rolling block design, a truly fascinating mechanism to see in action. "While Winchester's rifles utilized a sliding bolt moving toward and away from the chamber, their new shotgun had a bolt which duplicated the arc made by the lever in its movement. As the bolt slides upward into its closed position, a camming action is effected by forcing the rear portion of the bolt against the receiver... With a powder fouled chamber or shells which were oversize ... this was an important feature."

Indeed, that proved to be just the case with my 111-year old 10-gauge specimen when a slightly oversize brass shell required considerable force to extract. Black-powder paper shells

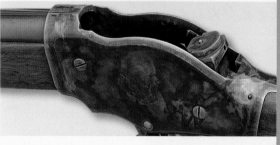

were no problem, and the gun accepted them with ease.

The 1887 was offered with a standard rolled-steel barrel (or Damascus for an additional $15 to $20). Barrels were full choked unless otherwise specified, and Winchester offered cylinder-bore and modified choke as an option. The 1887s had beautifully color case-hardened receivers and levers, and barrel lengths of 30 and 32 inches. Custom barrel lengths were offered and a short-barrel version was available for lawmen, guards and messengers. Most guard guns had a 22¼-inch barrel, making them imposing weapons.

In 1897 Winchester listed a Riot Gun variant described as follows: "The Winchester lever action 'Riot' gun is made with a 20-inch, rolled-steel barrel, cylinder-bore barrel, bored expressly to shoot buckshot... They are far superior to a revolver for shooting in the dark, where aim is uncertain, as a buckshot cartridge contains nine bullets to one contained by a revolver cartridge. The 'Riot' gun has the regular lever-action. The magazine holds five cartridges, which, with one in the chamber, makes a total of six at the command of the shooter."

A distinctive design with a profile similar to the Spencer rifle, the identifying marks of the 1887 are the Winchester address on the lower tang under the lever, the gauge stamped on the top of the barrel just forward of the receiver, and the serial number stamped on the bottom of the receiver just ahead of the lever. Early models also bore the Winchester proof mark "WP" inside an oval on the left side of the barrel. While the use of factory proof marks were inconsistent, every 1887 had the ornate Winchester Repeating Arms Co. monogram stamped into the left side of the receiver. The standard finish for the barrel and metal surfaces was bright blue. A handsome browned finish for the barrel was also offered as an option.

The Browning design was well conceived, sturdy and capable of handling heavy black-powder loads, but it left a couple of things to chance. There was no safety, and the semi-concealed hammer didn't project much above the breech-bolt.

Shouldering the hefty lever gun for an aimed shot reveals a standard brass-bead front sight, but once again there were options offered by Winchester. Customers could order nickel-silver front sights with a mid-bead. The rear sight was simply a notch in the forward part of the receiver, a holdover from the traditional side-by-side where shooters learned to sight down the centerline of the two barrels. Rounded semi-pistol grip stocks and a generous buttplate made the 1887 easier to handle. The factory also provided custom checkering on the fore-ends and pistol grip and select walnut stocks with varnished finish, but the majority of 1887s that were produced had standard oil-stained straight-grain walnut stocks.

The fore-end design is one of the model's most distinctive features. It's of two-piece construction divided by the barrel and magazine tube and held together with one screw on early models and two on later production. The two series also differed in the type of magazine retainer used. Early examples had a stud secured to the underside of the barrel with a screw holding the retainer cap in place. This was changed around serial number 28000, and by serial numbers above 30000 the design changeover had been fully integrated. The improved retainer used a steel band that partially encircled the barrel and was secured by a screw. A second screw passed completely through the end of the magazine. This later design was carried over to the Model 1901. The 1887 was discontinued

after approximately 64,855 had been produced, and was replaced by the 1901, which was manufactured through 1920.

The 1901 was only available in 10-gauge with a standard 32-inch barrel. There were no Riot variations, thus any short-barreled 1901s were cut down. Built to handle the new smokeless-powder cartridges (1887 models were black powder only), the 1901 came with a bright blue receiver, barrel and lever. The beautiful case-colored receiver was discontinued.

There were subtle changes in the 1901's design, particularly in the lever, which was now two pieces, and the addition of a trigger block, which prevented accidental discharge as the lever was being closed. Another new feature was a mechanically operated firing pin retractor. The choke type was now stamped on the left side of the barrel near the receiver, and the Winchester trademark moved to the upper tang. Proof marks were consistent and an address with patent dates and the 1901 designation and gauge were added to the top of the barrel. Serial numbers for the '01 series began at 64856—13,500 were produced.

My test guns—one built in 1892, the other in 1909—performed without problem with handloaded 10-gauge paper shells and No. 7½ shot. Heftier than a lever-action rifle, the Winchester 10-gauge isn't as agile to lever from the shoulder but is terrifically exciting to fire. At ranges of 25 feet the pattern was tight and one can only imagine the deadly accuracy with buckshot. Unfortunately, Winchester's hope that the legendary reputation of its lever-action rifles would rub off on its shotguns was unfulfilled. Sales to the public were never brisk, and Winchester itself created stiff competition for the 1887 with the introduction of the Browning-designed 1893 and 1897 slide-action shotguns—one of the most successful designs of the late 19th and early 20th century.

Classic Shotguns
Browning Auto-5

*"The best thing I ever made...":
John M. Browning's groundbreaking,
humpbacked, recoil-operated game-getter.*

In the fall of 1889, something extraordinary happened near Ogden, Utah. When the Ogden Rifle Club met for its weekly shoot, a small gallery assembled as Will Wright—a local marksman—came up to the firing line. Will leaned back to counterbalance the weight of his target rifle, obtained his sight picture and caressed the trigger.

A booming report echoed, and a clump of weeds downrange was blown flat by the muzzle blast. The gallery gazed intently toward the target, except for one elder of the Mormon church, whose attention was fixed on the clump of weeds. The elder was something of a marksman himself and a gunsmith to boot. But at the moment, the elder was oblivious to Wright's shot as he stared at the waving clump of weeds.

Seemingly insignificant events can alter history if the right person happens to notice and John M. Browning definitely noticed the unharnessed energy of a rifle shot that blew some weeds flat on a rifle range in Utah.

THE LEGENDARY RELIABILITY AND OVERALL SHOOTING
CHARACTERISTICS OF THE BROWNING A-5 ARE IMPRESSIVE.

By the next afternoon Browning and his brothers had devised a fully automatic firearm harnessing that energy. During the next 10 years, Browning would invent machine guns, semiautomatic pistols and one other gun that he himself called "The best thing I ever made..." When that gun finally went into production in 1903, it hit the market like a juggernaut as the Browning Automatic-5 shotgun.

On March 6, 1899, Browning sent a letter to T.G. Bennett of Winchester Repeating Arms saying he had an automatic shotgun ready and that he would come to New Haven to show it by the end of the month.

By 1899 Browning and Bennett had a business relationship going back 16 years to the time that Bennett had bought the rights to a single-shot rifle that was to become the Winchester Model 1885. Since then Winchester had purchased 44 rifle and shotgun designs from Browning.

So when Browning announced he had a prototype of an "automatic shotgun," Bennett gave him his full attention. But Bennett was not eager to buy this radical new firearm.

THE BROWNING A-5 (TOP) WENT INTO PRODUCTION IN 1903. THE NEAR-IDENTICAL REMINGTON MODEL 11 (BOTTOM) BEGAN PRODUCTION IN 1905 UNDER THE BROWNING PATENT. MINOR DIFFERENCES: NOTE THE DIFFERENCE IN THE CROSSBOLT SAFETY HEADS AND PISTOL-GRIP CONFIGURATIONS OF THE BROWNING (TOP) AND REMINGTON (BOTTOM) VERSIONS OF THE A-5.

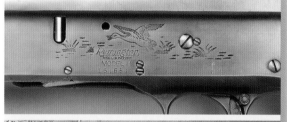

ALTHOUGH PLAINER IN APPEARANCE THAN THE BROWNING VERSION, THIS 16-GAUGE REMINGTON MODEL 11 NONETHELESS SPORTS ROLLED ENGRAVING ON THE RECEIVER. THE BROWNING A-5 SPORTS A MAGAZINE CUTOFF—A FEATURE LACKING ON THE REMINGTON MODEL 11.

From the perspective of the 21st century, it's hard to visualize how radical the Auto-5 was at the close of the 19th century. Arguably the most advanced repeating shotgun of the day was the Winchester Model 97, another Browning design. It was one of the bestsellers in the Winchester line, but it had more similarities to earlier 19th century arms than it did to the A-5. Its slide action resembled that of the Colt Lightning, and its external hammer was familiar to shooters of the day.

But the A-5 was ready to fire again as quickly as the shooter could pull the trigger. Light loads, heavy loads—it didn't matter. The A-5 could digest them all. It was also the first hammerless, solid-breech, multishot repeating shotgun ever seen.

Everything considered, the A-5 was too radical for a conservative businessman such as Bennett, and it put him in a bad position. If the gun proved to be a failure, it would be an expensive black eye for Winchester. If it were a success, it would, at best, rob from the sales of the lucrative Model 97. But if he rejected it and a major competitor began making it, Winchester would be relegated to the second tier of American gunmakers overnight. So Bennett stalled for more than two years. Then in January 1902, following an angry meeting with Bennett, Browning finally collected his prototypes and walked out.

After Browning left, he called Marcellus Hartley, president of Remington Arms, who invited Browning to meet with him that afternoon. While Browning sat waiting in Remington's reception room, the telephone rang with the news that Hartley had died from a heart attack a few min-

THE RECOIL-OPERATED A-5 STRIPS DOWN QUICKLY FOR EASY CLEANING AND MAINTENANCE, WHICH IS A MUST FOR ANY HARD-DUTY FIELD AUTO, PARTICULARLY A WATERFOWL GUN.

utes earlier.

Browning had but one choice left. He traveled to Europe to offer his shotgun to Belgium's Fabrique Nationale. A few years earlier, Browning had licensed FN to manufacture a .32-caliber pistol, and sales of the new handgun had rescued the company from bankruptcy.

STEVE COMUS LIKES THE HANDLING QUALITIES OF HIS WELL-USED 20-GAUGE BROWNING A-5, WHICH HE USED TO TAKE A "GRAND SLAM" OF QUAIL SPECIES.

When FN officials saw the prototype, they were exuberant. The new shotgun would be FN's entry into the hunting market. After weeks of discussion and testing, Browning signed a contract granting FN exclusive rights to manufacture and sell the gun. By the fall of 1903 FN had begun production of the A-5.

Confident that his new shotgun would be successful, Browning placed an order for 10,000 Auto-5s, which were to be marked with the name of a nonexistent firm, Browning Automatic Arms Company, and would be sold in the U.S. through a major distributor. Browning's confidence was borne out as all 10,000 guns were sold within a year.

When the U.S. enacted restrictive tariffs on foreign goods in 1904, Browning concluded that the tariff would make foreign manufacture impractical. So, after negotiations with FN, he arranged for Remington to produce and sell the new shotgun. Remington produced Browning's design as its Model 11. The Remington 11 differed from the FN version in its use of the old-style carrier without the quick-load feature and the lack of a magazine cut-off.

FN continued to manufacture the A-5 even though its reception in Europe was decidedly less enthusiastic than in America. But FN found a much more receptive market for the A-5 outside Europe. In India, Africa and elsewhere, the Browning gained a reputation as a reliable multipurpose arm capable of bagging sizeable animals with buckshot or slugs and proved equally effective on waterfowl and upland game.

By the 1920s the A-5 was turning in stellar performances at live-bird shoots and clay-bird competitions. A world trap record was set with an A-5 at the 1924 Olympics.

The A-5 marked its 100th birthday in 2003 having been manufactured with little variation by Fabrique Nationale, Remington, Savage, Franchi, Breda, Miroku and others. More than 2.5 million have been made under the Browning name alone. My 16-gauge Remington Model 11 bears a serial number well into seven figures, although this is not a reliable indication of total production. Best estimates indicate that in excess of 3 million A-5s are in the hands of shooters worldwide. The three Browning patent guns featured here include A-5s in 12-gauge and 20-gauge owned by a friend of mine and my Remington 11. All three appear to be of postwar manufacture.

Both Brownings are embellished with sparse, elegant engraving in what has come to be known as the "Browning style." On the left side of both receivers the name "Browning" is proudly displayed surmounting a tiny likeness of John Browning set in a simple oval—all embedded in a delicate floral pattern. The plainer Remington sports rolled engraving depicting a running pheasant on the right side of the receiver and a duck rising off a marsh on the left. All three guns are stocked with richly hued walnut that would have been called plain a few decades ago and are hand-checkered in a point pattern of about 18 lpi.

After more than 100 years the humpbacked Browning A-5, in all its variations, still holds its own with the best that 21st century gunmakers can produce. Like many Browning designs, the A-5 is timeless.

Although he is relatively obscure today, Andrew Burgess was one of the 19th Century's premier firearms designers.

Working for Whitney, Marlin, Colt and finally himself, Andrew Burgess accumulated 599 firearms patents—about ⅔ as many as the great John Moses Browning. Many are still in use today.

The prolific designer's professional life began as an apprentice photographer to Matthew Brady in 1855 and he worked throughout the Civil War. While observing and perhaps photographing the Franco-Prussian war, Burgess became interested in the design of repeating firearms. His first successful design, the Model 1878 Whitney/Burgess repeating rifle chambered for the .45-70, satisfied the "Holy Grail" of the 1870s—a repeating rifle for the Government cartridge. That it did not sell up to its expectations were due more to the marketing failure of Whitney, rather than an inherent problems with the Burgess design.

The Burgess-designed Marlin Model 1881 was truly the first successful repeating rifle chambered for the .45-70 cartridge and was an immediate success. In ensuing years, Burgess designed guns for Colt and Whitney as well as marketing many other firearms related patents. One of Burgess' most important patents was for the 45-degree drop-lock locking system that many of the day's designers modified for use in their own firearms. This system shows up in the Colt Lightning rifle, the 1886 Whitney, the 1886 Mannlicher straight-pull rifle, the Winchester 1893 shotgun, the Burgess shotgun and a host of Marlin slide-action rifles.

Burgess derived the majority of his income from royalties. By the late 1880s, Winchester bought Whitney and shut it down; Colt dropped his lever gun in favor of the Eliot designed pump and Burgess' income was falling. He decided to manufacture guns himself and The Burgess Gun Co. in Buffalo, New York began manufacturing his pistol-grip pump-action shotgun in 1893.

The Burgess shotgun has several handling and design characteristics that make it unique. By placing the action mechanism in the grip, Burgess allowed for a natural in-line motion

Burgess Repeating Shotgun

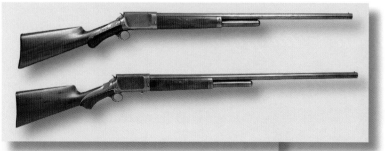

THERE ARE TWO DIFFERENT MODELS OF SPORTING SHOTGUNS FROM THE BURGESS GUN CO. TOP IS AN EARLY MODEL WITH FAR MORE DROP IN THE COMB, A ROUND, HARD RUBBER PUMP PISTOL-GRIP AND ITS ACTION RELEASE BEHIND THE TRIGGER GUARD. BELOW IS THE LATER MODEL WITH HIGH-COMB STOCK, WOODEN PISTOL GRIP, FORWARD ACTION RELEASE AND ROLL MARKINGS.

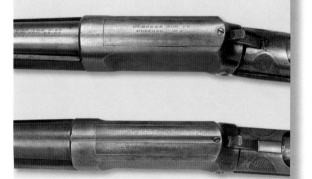

IN WHAT MUST HAVE BEEN A VERY EXPENSIVE PROCEDURE EVEN BY 19TH CENTURY STANDARDS, ALL FACTORY MARKINGS ARE ENGRAVED ON THE EARLY MODEL BURGESS GUNS UP TO THE MIDDLE OF THE GUN'S PRODUCTION. LATER MODELS HAD CONVENTIONAL ROLL-DIE MARKINGS (BOTTOM).

EARLY GUNS HAD EXTENSIVE PATENT AND ADDRESS MARKINGS ENGRAVED ON THE BARREL. LATER GUNS USED A SIMPLE ROLL DIE MARKING ON THE BOTTOM OF THE MAGAZINE GATE.

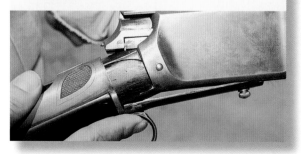

during the feed/eject cycle that leaves the left hand free to keep the gun steady and on target. It is also completely ambidextrous. Other benefits of this design include a neutral balance that allows the gun to feel alive when it is swung on a target and a takedown system that is simple and sturdy.

Although production of all models of Burgess shotguns are estimated at a few thousand, some changes in the design occurred. Early sporting models featured a low comb stock with quite a bit of drop—as did many contemporary shotguns—and a checkered hard rubber pistol grip. One unusual feature is the extensive hand-engraved legends on the early guns. Later guns had conventional roll-engraved markings, wooden pistol grips and a higher comb stock that is similar to today's style. The action release was moved from outside of the triggerguard at the back to the front of the triggerguard on the inside. Similar to its far more successful rival—the 1897 Winchester—the Burgess utilizes its hammer's half-cock notch as the safety.

The Burgess has one main fault, however. Although it has a strong, sound system of action lock-up, it is a relatively weak design. The receiver is cut completely away at the back for the breechblock and completely away at the bottom for the tongue-and-groove takedown system. By comparison, the venerable '97 Winchester has a fairly solid receiver. Burgess understood his gun's weakness and planned for it accordingly. Choosing not to make his own barrels, Burgess bought the best quality Damascus barrels available in 11-gauge. They were chambered for 12-gauge and full-choked versions have a .040-inch constriction. The oversized bore (today we call it back-boring) helps reduce the pressure on the mechanism

WHEN THE ACTION IS CLOSED, THE BREECHBLOCK IS LOCKED TO THE RECEIVER. PRESSING UP ON THE ACTION RELEASE BUTTON LOCATED INSIDE THE TRIGGER GUARD RELEASES THE BREECHBLOCK FOR UNLOADING OF THE GUN. THE KNURLED NUT ON THE MAGAZINE GATE IS NOT ORIGINAL, BUT A LATER GUNSMITH'S REPAIR.

while the tremendous constriction throws dense patterns with low velocity black powder loads.

For this test, I wanted to shoot both guns, but the bore condition of the 1st Model made me think twice. Even the best quality Damascus barrels can let go eventually and the bore of this one was rough. The 2nd Model's bore looked good and this was the one we shot. After shooting a few patterns and chronographing the loads, I was pleased enough with the performance to plan hunting with this shotgun. First, though, a trip to Moore & Moore Sporting Clays in Tujunga, California, on a day wet enough to not start any brush fires. The lively feel of the gun caused me to miss mightily at first, yet it became an asset after learning to control it. My shooting buddy had to stand about five feet to starboard to see if a hit had been made due to the voluminous cloud of white smoke from the 3¾-drams of black powder. After 10 or 20 rounds to get acclimated, I was able to record my usual meager sporting clays score that habitually hovers in the mid 70s. Still, I was confident enough in the gun now to take it to the hunting fields.

During dove season, I finished my dove limit with the Burgess gun by only taking shots farther than 30 yards to ensure that enough dove would be left to eat. One surprisingly pleasant aspect of black powder shotshells is the remarkably low recoil. There was less apparent felt recoil than from the 1-ounce dove loads I had been firing from my Beretta 390. The Burgess shotgun is one of the more fun guns I have shot and handles differently than any other gun I've used. It is still quite capable of taking game.

Although the mechanism may not have survived in the smokeless powder era due to its lack of inherent action strength, it is a shame that it died so early. Andrew Burgess sold his company to Winchester in 1899. Winchester promptly closed the factory and locked away the patents. Thus ended the manufacture of one of history's more interesting shotguns. Burgess lived on working on automatic weapons patents for nine years, dying quietly in St. Augustine, Florida on December 19, 1908.

TO LOAD THE BURGESS SHOTGUN, OPEN THE ACTION AND THE SLIP THE SHELLS INTO THE MAGAZINE. TURN THE GUN OVER, DROP A SHELL ONTO THE CARRIER AND CLOSE THE ACTION.

THE ONLY SAFETY IS THE HALF-COCK NOTCH OF THE HAMMER, SIMILAR TO WINCHESTER'S LEGENDARY MODEL 1897 SHOTGUN. IT IS FAST AND CONVENIENT.

THE MAGAZINE SHELL STOP WAS LOCATED IN THE BARREL/MAGAZINE GROUP, ALLOWING THE BROKEN DOWN GUN TO BE CARRIED WITH THE MAGAZINE LOADED. ALTHOUGH NOT A VALUABLE FEATURE IN A SPORTING GUN, IT WAS IN THE FOLDING RIOT GUN.

A COMMON DENOMINATOR IN BURGESS DESIGNED GUNS IS THE SMOOTHNESS OF THE ACTION, AND THE SHOTGUN MAY THE SMOOTHEST OF ALL. IT IS EFFORTLESS TO WORK DURING FEEDING AND EXTRACTION. BRASS SHELLS WORK BEST BECAUSE TODAY'S FOLDED CRIMP HULLS ARE A BIT TOO LONG TO EJECT CLEANLY UNLESS THERE IS ANOTHER ROUND ON THE CARRIER TO FORCE IT OUT OF THE EJECTION PORT.

Classic Shotguns

Winchester Model 42

THE WINCHESTER
MODEL 42
by
NED SCHWING

with technical assistance by
Don "Duck" Combs

Built to scale:

This diminutive pump-action shotgun

still represents the Holy Grail for .410 fanatics.

Whenever the discussion would turn to .410s, "Uncle" Bill Fleming's face would light up at the mere mention of the Model 42 pump. In fact, "Uncle" Bill, our local shotgun expert, was responsible for me getting my own. Skeet Models represented the bulk of what was available on the market during the two decades that Fleming and I haunted shotgun ranges together. But I wanted a hunting Model 42—no frills, no rib, just the honest, basic gun. Finally, I found it. And, frankly, the only reason I haven't bothered to look for more is that this specific shotgun does everything a .410 field gun should—or could—do.

I remember when the Model 42 was in production. Most hunters in my part of western Ohio considered it an extravagance. After all, Model 42s cost as much—or more—than a comparable Model 12. And everyone back in the 1950s just knew that there was nothing better than a 12-gauge with a 30-inch full-

MODEL 42 ENTHUSIASTS ARE DOWNRIGHT FANATICAL IN THEIR LOVE FOR WHAT MANY CONSIDER TO BE THE FINEST .410 EVER MADE.

choke barrel. Even though I had yet to develop my smallbore fetish, I did look longingly at the sole Model 42 on the rack at Shorty's Sport Shop.

The Model 42 is more than just a scaled-down Model 12. But although there are many differences in the actions between both of those classic pumps, cosmetically, they're similar. During the Model 42's 30-year production run (1933 to 1963), it's safe to say that there were about 160,000 made.

The gun was the brainchild of designer William Roemer. He began work on the Model 42 in 1928, but production didn't begin until the depths of the Great Depression. Actually, the Model 42 came out a little later than it might have. John Olin wanted to time the little pumpgun's debut with that of Western Cartridge Company's 3-inch .410 Super-X shotshell. Originally, the Model 42 was designed to handle 2½-inch shells and had to be redesigned to handle the longer ones as well (although some Skeet Model 42s had 2½-inch chambers). The Model 42s magazine holds five 3-inch shells, which makes it a

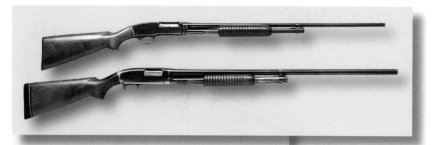

PUMPGUN PERFECTION PAIRED UP: THE MODEL 42 (TOP) OBVIOUSLY RESEMBLES THE BIGGER MODEL 12, BUT THERE ARE MANY INTERNAL DIFFERENCES BETWEEN THE TWO.

THE MODEL 42'S SLIM RECEIVER (LEFT) TESTIFIES TO ITS "THOROUGHBRED .410" LINEAGE. SHOWN NEXT TO IT IS THE RECEIVER OF A 12-GAUGE MODEL 12 FOR COMPARISON.

THE TAKEDOWN RELEASE IS DISTINCTIVELY "MODEL 12-ISH," AS OPPOSED TO THE SCREW-OFF MAGAZINE TUBE CAP OF THE REMINGTON 870.

DESIGNED BY WILLIAM ROEMER, THE MODEL 42 WAS INTRODUCED IN 1933 AND STAYED IN THE WINCHESTER CATALOG FOR 30 YEARS.

six-shooter if one round is loaded into the chamber and the magazine is filled. My gun, following the hunting regulations, has a dowel plug, limiting the magazine capacity to two since it finds itself in the duck blind from time to time.

The Model 42 weighs around six pounds, depending upon barrel length, whether there is a rib and things like that. It was designed from the ground up to be a .410. That's probably why it's so universally revered. The little pump pretty much stands alone in that regard.

There were several major categories and grades, starting with the Standard Grade produced throughout the entire production span (except for the WWII period, when some guns may have been cobbled together from existing parts), the Skeet Model (1934 to 1963), the Trap Grade (1934 to 1939), the Trap-Grade Skeet (1934 to 1939), the Deluxe (about 1950 to 1963) and the Pigeon Grade (1930s to 1950s).

Generally speaking, the lower grades had corncob-style slide handles and smooth, full or semipistol-grip stocks. The higher grades featured differing checkering designs on the slide handle and grip. Barrels ranged from plain and matted to raised rib and vent rib. Hard-rubber buttplates were standard, but virtually any kind of buttplate or pad was available on special order. In fact, one of the interesting things about most Winchester firearms made during that same period is that the factory shipped all kinds of special-order guns, which means there are many nonstandard specimens at large.

For a time Winchester also offered the Model 42 with a Cutts compensator (generally a skeet-gun feature). Barrels generally were 26 or 28 inches long and were choked improved-cylinder, modified, full or skeet. Steel grip caps were standard on the later guns.

The Model 42 was a natural for embellishment. Factory-engraving levels included 42-1, 42-1A, 42-2B, 42-1C, 42-2, 42-3, 42-4 and 42-5. This span went from "upgraded" to "really fancy" and covered some awesome wood and superb checkering.

In 1933 the Model 42 made instant history in the skeet world by setting the .410-bore long-run world's record. Pumpguns are almost extinct among competitive skeet shooters these days, but they were major players long ago. Skeet was different then, as former skeet world champ Robert Stack used to explain to me as we went from one station to another. He used to recall fondly how the game changed when shooters could go from a low-gun to a high-gun mount before calling for targets. But that's another story.

Because the Model 42 is light in both weight and recoil, it has been used a lot by beginners. During its production run, more "serious" hunters opted for bigger guns with greater shot payloads. The Model 42 may have been cute, but it probably wasn't taken all that seriously as a field gun.

And there lies the reality of the .410. The myth is that it's a beginner's gun. In reality, it's an expert's dream.

Although I admire the fancier-grade Model 42s, for me, the pure beauty of the gun best resides in the plain-barrel Standard Grade. Form, function, handling characteristics—everything comes together poetically into one of the finest pump shotguns ever made.

The serial number of my Model 42 is in the 97XXX range, meaning it's a 1950s gun. With its 28-inch modified barrel, it's a death ray on quail or dove. Conscious thought isn't required to hit with it; it seems to shoulder itself, swing onto target and hit, all in a smooth, continuous move. Most of what I use my Model 42 for calls for a steady diet of 2½-inch reloads featuring one-half ounce of 7½s.

A right-to-left-crossing whitewing with a tailwind may as well dive-bomb the game bag because that's where he's heading. The same holds true for flushing Gambel's and scaled quail. The Model 42 gets on them so quickly and effortlessly that I am able to engage the bird a full five yards closer than I can with a larger, heavier gun. So much for the .410 "disadvantage."

Could anything be better? Only the same gun with a full choke, perhaps, but I'd have

THE AUTHOR'S WELL-USED WINCHESTER MODEL 42 SEES THE MAJORITY OF ITS ACTION ON WHITE-WING DOVE AND GAMBEL'S QUAIL IN ARIZONA.

THE AUTHOR'S STANDARD GRADE MODEL 42 SPORTS THE DISTINCTIVE "CORNCOB" PUMP HANDLE. SKEET GRADE GUNS FEATURED MORE STREAMLINED CHECKERED PUMP HANDLES.

THE INTRODUCTION OF THE MODEL 42 COINCIDED WITH THAT OF THE 3-INCH .410 SUPER-X SHOT-SHELL (FAR RIGHT). IT'S PROBABLY A BETTER CHOICE FOR HUNTING THAN THE 2½-INCH .410 (CENTER). BOTH .410S, HOWEVER, ARE DWARFED BY THE 12 GAUGE (LEFT).

to think about that for a while. Although the gun cycles 3-inch shells marginally better and smoother than 2½ inchers, I haven't found a need to use 3-inch shells on anything short of waterfowl (and Bismuth .410s are awesome duck medicine).

And could any hunting scene be more classic than a crisp, fall Midwest day with beagles, cottontails and a Model 42? As long as there are hunters who appreciate something a little different, a little more fun, the Model 42 will live forever.

Classic Shotguns
Ithaca Model 37 Featherlight

Slick handling characteristics and Browning's eminently sensible bottom-ejecting design are hallmarks of this classic pump.

The year 1972 was a pretty fair one on the trap line for Dad and me. When we sold the last of our furs at the end of the season our take was a little over $300—of which I got a half share. I thought it was more money than any 12-year-old kid had ever seen, and I knew just what to do with it: Buy a shotgun.

Dad handled the transaction, and not too long before my first hunting season he came home with the gun that was to become my partner for more than 30 years: an Ithaca Model 37 Featherlight in 16-gauge. He bought it used, and, as I recall, it cost me a little over $100. Even back then the gun didn't have much blueing, but the action was slick as butter, and it flew to my shoulder like it had wings. Later, a bit of research told me that my particular shotgun—serial number 969XXX— was manufactured by Ithaca in early 1967.

The Ithaca quickly became my pride and

joy, and I was tempted by no other. I loved the "ringtail" fore-end and the scenes of ringnecks and winging ducks engraved on the flat receiver. I loved the Raybar front bead, and I loved the way that fast little pump could rap out shots.

The Ithaca accounted for my first squirrel, dropped from the raggedy, silver surface of a shagbark hickory one October evening. My first rabbit rolled to its thundering report that same fall, and a year later two quick shots knocked down a gaudy, cackling ringneck.

There have been other firsts with that gun—turkey, dove, duck (lead was still legal then), various species of quail—and the Ithaca is still my favorite choice for small game.

Like many of our great gun designs, the M37 was invented by John M. Browning, who patented the bottom-eject shotgun in 1915. Remington was first to produce the design, scaling it to 20-gauge proportions and introducing it as the Model 17 in 1921.

Remington eventually tired of the design, and the Ithaca Gun Company under Lou Smith picked it up when the patent expired.

A BOTTOM-EJECTION PORT HELPS KEEP TWIGS AND MUCK OUT OF THE ACTION, AND IT'S AN EQUAL-OPPORTUNITY DESIGN FOR LEFT-HANDED SHOOTERS.

THE MINIMALIST ADORNMENT ON THE RECEIVER OF THE AUTHOR'S MODEL 37 HAS AN INDUSTRIAL-STRENGTH CHARM ALL ITS OWN.

A MODEL 37 HALLMARK IS THE DISTINCTIVE AND EASY-TO-GRASP "RINGTAIL" FORE-END.

AFTER RE-STOCKING HIS MODEL 37, THE AUTHOR WAS LOATHE TO LOSE THE ORIGINAL GRIP CAP, SO HE REINSTALLED IT.

EASY DISASSEMBLY: SLIDE THE PIN OUT OF THE MAGAZINE CAP, GIVE THE CAP A FEW CLOCKWISE TURNS, AND THEN TWIST THE BARREL COUNTER-CLOCKWISE TO FREE IT.

Ithaca beefed up the gun to handle 12-gauge shells, and the Model 37 made its debut in 1937. A 16-gauge version followed a year later and was the first to use the moniker "Featherlight," an apt description for a shotgun that weighed only six pounds.

As the story goes, Smith was an avid fox hunter—not a member of the dressed-in-red equine set but rather the kind of guy who followed his hounds on foot over hill and dale for miles at a time. He wanted a lighter gun and reckoned he wasn't the only American hunter who might like a scattergun that didn't feel like it weighed a ton at the end of the day.

The M37 Featherlight was offered in all three popular gauges with the introduction of the 20 in 1939. It's a hammerless takedown that's incredibly quick to disassemble; simply slide out the pin in the magazine cap, give the cap a few turns clockwise, and then twist the barrel counterclockwise to free it.

Barrels were offered in 26, 28 and 30 inches (12-gauge only for the latter), and they could be had in one of the three most popular chokes: full, modified and improved cylinder. Gun weights range from 5¾ to 7½ pounds depending on gauge and barrel length. The magazine holds four rounds, and the wooden plug in my Featherlight is labeled "For 12 and 16 ga. repeater to conform with 3 shot federal migratory bird law" and is imprinted with instructions for installing the plug.

The Featherlight stock is nothing fancy, just a checkered pistol grip, and the fore-end was either checkered or grooved depending on year of manufacture.

The M37 spawned dozens of variations over the years: commemoratives, magnums, skeet and trap models, the venerable Deer Slayer slugger and even law enforcement and trench guns. The M37 Military is the rarest of all trench shotguns. It sported a highly polished, blue finish and had a blued, ventilated handguard onto which a bayonet could be fastened. Less than 1,500 of these were ordered by the War Department in 1941. A later version, produced in the Vietnam era, was Parkerized.

On the other end of the spectrum were M37s such as the $1,000 Grade and $5,000 Grade, which were lavishly engraved and gold-inlaid affairs with select walnut stocks. The former was produced in the late 1930s, the latter from 1947 to 1967.

In all, more than 2 million Model 37s were produced between 1937 and 1984, and one of the reasons for their popularity was the bottom-ejection design, which is less susceptible to dirt finding its way inside the receiver. And in the unlikely event of a shell rupture, gases and debris are directed downward, away from the shooter's face. Similarly, spent hulls don't pass in front of the eyes—an attribute that makes the M37 very appealing to southpaws.

I've shot a lot of pumps over the years, and I've never used one that works as fast or as easily as does an M37 with a few years under its belt. The fore-end doesn't twist or bind and, if kept in good working order, will slide down the magazine tube of its own volition once the action-release ratchet is depressed.

Yes, I know the measure of good wingshot isn't how fast he can empty his gun at a fleeting target. But it's nice to know if you need that second or third shot, you can get it off before the bird or bunny is in the next county.

For all its advantages and its popularity, though, sales of the M37 could not stave off Ithaca Gun Company's financial woes, and the firm closed its doors in 1986. The following year, the Ithaca Acquisition Company rescued the defunct gunmaker, and in honor of the year of the manufacturer's resurrection and the gun's 50th anniversary, the Model 37 was renamed the Model 87 when production resumed.

The tenure of the Ithaca Acquisition Company was relatively short; by 1995 it had been forced into bankruptcy just like its

THE AUTHOR AND HIS ITHACA PROWL PENNSYL-VANIA GROUSE COVER. HE BELIEVES THAT THE MODEL 37'S WEIGHT AND HANDLING CHARACTERISTICS MAKE IT THE ULTIMATE UPLAND GUN.

predecessor. A few months later, however, a group of investors formed Ithaca Gun Company LLC, keeping the Ithaca name—and the guns—alive. Thankfully, the firm restored the designation of its trademark bottom-ejection shotgun back to the Model 37, and a 16-gauge version returned in 1999.

Today there are a dozen M37 variants running the gamut from a nifty English-stocked upland model to special-purpose shotguns for deer, turkey and waterfowl. The New Classic, a spitting image of the original M37, is available in all three gauges and traces its parentage back to the era when my Featherlight was made, but adds modern touches such as interchangeable chokes.

I've seen and handled the modern Classic, and I can't tell any difference between it and my M37—except the new one is a lot prettier. As I mentioned, the blueing on my old gun is largely gone, giving the metal a silvery-brown appearance. The bottom of the receiver has a good ding in it, the result of a tumble taken in rocky central Pennsylvania while hunting turkey. Gone is the original Raybar sight. After I'd knocked out my second plastic orange insert by banging it against a tree, a gunsmith soldered on an oversize silver bead. The factory stock, which was cut down significantly to accommodate a short 12-year-old's arms, was replaced in the late 1970s, but I retained the grip cap and buttplate that came with the original.

Many times I've considered refurbishing my Ithaca, reblueing it or maybe even having the barrel threaded for interchangeable choke tubes. But then I take it out of the gun safe to go hunting or to wipe down the metal, and I realize any such "improvements" would ruin the gun. That Model 37 and I are growing old together, and refinishing the gun would be like me dyeing my hair to cover up the gray.

Index